Girls and Juvenile Justice

"*Girls and Juvenile Justice* offers an original and insightful analysis of the distinctive character of female delinquency. Davis show how family responses to adolescent troubles and resistance to control, rather than crime-like delinquent behavior per se, may move girls from ghetto and barrio families and neighborhoods into the juvenile justice system. Drawing on rich qualitative interview and observational data, she identifies the perspectives and concerns of incarcerated delinquent girls, tracing their familial and institutional careers as they are brought to juvenile court, adapt to a therapeutically oriented reform school, and are released back to their families and communities. A sensitive and moving study of critical processes in contemporary responses to troubled adolescents!"

—**Robert M. Emerson**, Professor Emeritus and Research Professor, University of California, Los Angeles, USA

"The much-needed conversation this book provides has great value in the field of criminology, where a focus on girls and their lives is often absent, excluded, and trivialized. Davis offers her readers insight into and understanding of girls who are in trouble with the law, both before and after incarceration. In this way, she "connects the dots" in female delinquents' pathways to justice involvement and offers a rare glimpse of the complex processes and relationships that encompass their lives."

—**Lisa Pasko**, Ph.D., Associate Professor, Department of Sociology and Criminology, University of Denver, USA

"Rich with the voices of adolescent urban girls involved in the justice system and the professionals who work with them, *Girls and Juvenile Justice* explores both the causes of the behavior that led to this involvement and society's reaction to that behavior. In creating this vivid portrait, Davis increases our understanding of the ideas and values that ground both the girls' choices and the institutional ways of addressing those choices. Davis argues that the girls actually fully accept mainstream values; that current therapeutic approaches ignore the role of the hierarchical structures of class, race/ethnicity and gender in creating their "undesirable" behaviors; and that such approaches, in fact, reinforce those hierarchies. Because her original analysis includes specific recommendations, this book will not only advance the theoretical discussions of scholars, but should also inform the practices of those in various professional roles within the juvenile justice system."

—**Judith Rollins**, Professor emerita, Wellesley College, USA, Author of *Between Women*

Carla P. Davis

Girls and Juvenile Justice

Power, Status, and the Social Construction of Delinquency

Carla P. Davis
Beloit College
Beloit, Wisconsin, USA

ISBN 978-3-319-42844-4   ISBN 978-3-319-42845-1   (eBook)
DOI 10.1007/978-3-319-42845-1

Library of Congress Control Number: 2016956448

Cover illustration: Cristina Lucero / Alamy Stock Photo

Printed on acid-free paper

This Palgrave Macmillan imprint is published by Springer Nature
The registered company is Springer International Publishing AG
The registered company address is: Gewerbestrasse 11, 6330 Cham, Switzerland

Acknowledgments

There are a number of people whom I would like to thank. First, I would like to thank Yunuen Rodriguez. I am grateful for her encouragement and enthusiasm for the book. I am grateful to her for spending so many hours/months in conversations, listening to me flesh out the meanings in the data. I am also grateful to Liz Young for our discussions fleshing out the meanings in the data. I would like to thank Christina Czuhajewski and Margaret Cress for their comments and assistance locating literature for Chap. 4. I am grateful for the enthusiasm of Gabrielle Gonzales. I would like to thank Katy Pinto for her comments on Chap. 4—and for being such a supportive friend. Thank you to Judith Rollins for comments on Chap. 6. I am grateful to Robert Emerson for his comments on earlier versions of Chaps. 3 and 5 and for giving me a solid foundation in ethnographic field research methods. I am also grateful to Tom McBride for his comments on Chap. 4, editing initial drafts of Chaps. 6 and 7 and for his encouragement and praise for the manuscript. Finally, I would like to thank all of the girls who participated in this study for letting me into their lives and simultaneously deepening my life. I am eternally grateful.

Contents

1

Introduction

MIRANDA: I done took pills like—um—five—six different times. I was just depressed—I was tired—what the fuck is up with living—if god—what the hell—god *supposedly*—wants us to be happy and take care of us—then what the hell—he can work miracles—he can do anything—where the hell he at?—why the hell he ain't helping me?—so it's like obviously—I guess he's not there. Like now—I know he's there, but I have no faith in him at all. I have no faith in God. And it's just like *whatever*. Fuck life and—um—what's the reason of livin'?

This narrative reflects a pattern of the overwhelming sense of hopelessness felt by girls in the juvenile justice system. Over the last few decades, the presence of girls in the criminal justice system has prompted a plethora of research. However, previous studies struggle to theorize the relationship between the girls' marginalized status in society and their presence in the juvenile justice system. The struggle to theorize the relationship between marginalization and girls' presence in the system is connected to two common practices: positing gender as the primary factor of social relations in the girls' lives, with race and class as mere additive dimensions; and conceptualizing gender as a dichotomously constructed variable expressing universal, essential differences between men and women.

© The Author(s) 2017
C.P. Davis, *Girls and Juvenile Justice*,
DOI 10.1007/978-3-319-42845-1_1

These interconnected practices contribute to the continued conception of gender as an individual attribute rather than a structure of resources, status, and power intertwined with structures of race/ethnicity, and class. Conceptualizing gender, race/ethnicity, and class as systems of resources, power, and status is critical to delineating the dialectic between structure and agency.

This book examines the lives of girls in the juvenile justice system in the context of gender, race/ethnicity, and class as simultaneous, intersecting structures of resources, status, and power. It examines the link between subjective inner consciousness (ideas, thoughts, emotions, attitudes) and the objective material world. Examining the girls' lives within this context illuminates how the girls' actions may be seen as attempts to gain a sense of power and status from their marginalized positions. In essence, this study asks, 'how does social marginalization shape how the girls make sense of and navigate their daily lives?'

A significant part of navigating daily life is about how people make sense of the myriad circumstances they encounter that potentially rob them of a sense of dignity. People manage these devaluing experiences by rationalizing them in a way that accords them at least a modicum of dignity. How one crafts and manages this sense of dignity is largely dependent upon the resources available. This is particularly critical for those at the bottom of the race, class, gender hierarchy who are keenly aware of their discredited status as they navigate their daily lives. Finding ways to maintain even a modicum of a sense of dignity is crucial to finding reason to continue existing in a world that denies them humanity and fails to acknowledge the realities of their existence. This book illuminates how in a world that accords them diminished power and status, Black and Brown girls draw upon dominant ideals to navigate and make sense of their worlds in a way that accords them at least a *sense* of status. In essence, these chapters are about institutional processes of negotiating status and power, and the social construction of identity within these processes.

Production of Knowledge and the Challenges of Conceptualizing Gender

Feminist theorists criticized the earliest studies attempting to explain girls' delinquency for drawing upon existing studies of boys' delinquency. However, the trouble was not that these early studies drew upon theories used to explain boys' delinquency; rather, it was that they drew upon the underlying problematic conceptions of gender embedded in those theories. Some of the most prevalent early studies attempted to apply Strain Theory, Social Learning Theory, and Masculinity Theory.

Ruth Morris (1964) was one of the first to apply Strain Theory to girls. She theorized that 'obstacles to economic power status are more likely to lead to delinquency in boys while obstacles to maintaining positive affective relationships are more likely to lead to delinquency in girls.' (83). In theorizing such, Morris adapted the underlying conception of gender as a dichotomously constructed individual attribute expressing universal, essential differences between men and women. She neglected to recognize gender as a structure comprised of resources, status, and power intersecting with structures of race and class. Morris failed to consider that perhaps economic power status might also lead to a greater likelihood of delinquency in girls as well. She also seemed not to consider that if girls seemed to be more interested in affective relationships, perhaps this might be connected in some way to attaining status or power.

Ruth Morris also applied Social Learning/Differential Association Theory to girls in attempting to explain girls' seemingly greater conformity reflected in lower rates of delinquency for girls. She theorized that 'there is a relative absence of a deviant subculture for female delinquents, and absence of subcultural as well as cultural support for female delinquency' (Morris 1965: 251). In applying social learning theory, Morris again posits gender as a primary dichotomous organizing factor without considering how gender intersects with race and class. Conceptualizing gender as the product of sex-role socialization inevitably leads to focusing on girls' actions in the context of conformity or deviance to gender roles reflected in stereotypical notions of masculinity or femininity. This conceptualization of gender leads to the conclusion that gender plays such an enormous role simply because men are different from women. Masculinity theory epitomizes conceptualizing gender as a primary dichotomously constructed individual attribute that is the product of sex-role socialization. Masculinity Theory hypothesizes that masculinity—reflected in qualities that exemplify maleness (daring, toughness, aggression)—provides the basis for motive in delinquency. Studies attempting to apply masculinity theories to women measured 'levels' of masculine/feminine traits in girls/women in an attempt to determine whether there was a correlation between these male traits and delinquency (Cullen, Golder and Cullen 1979; Loy and Norland 1981; Thornton and James 1979; Widom 1979). In essence, early studies applying existing 'boys' theories are problematic in that they conceptualized gender as an individual attribute expressing essential differences between men and women. As such, they treat gender as comprising of 'doing' masculinity and femininity rather than as a system of resources, power, and status.

The impact of feminism led to an increase in the focus on women and crime. However, feminist theories continued the practice of conceptualizing gender as a primary, dichotomously constructed individual attribute. For example, in Women's Liberation Theory, Adler (1975) argued that liberation and economic gains led to women's empowerment, thus promoting 'equality' in crime. According to Adler, economic gains caused women to engage in more crime, specifically more serious or violent crime. The primary problem with this theory was that by not considering how gender is a structure intersecting with systems of race and class, it contradicted the well-understood inverse relationship between resources/power/status, and crime and delinquency. In other words, it missed the fact that an increase in the ratio of crime/delinquency is a function of a *lack* of resources, status, and power, not a gain. It also missed the fact that women did not actually obtain enough in the way of resources, status, and power to change the power structure. In essence, Liberation Theory continued the practicing of conceptualizing gender as a dichotomous, individual characteristic resulting from conformity or deviance to gender roles rather than in terms of hierarchies of resources, status, and power. These conceptualizations view the girls' actions in terms of 'doing gender' which is, in essence, a matter of whether women or girls are portraying masculine or feminine behaviors.

Another later development of the impact of feminism was a call for a broader understanding of how lives are 'gendered' by starting with an examination of girls' lives (Chesney-Lind 1989, 1997, 1999) rather than theorizing from above. Daly and Chesney-Lind (1988) defined a feminist perspective as 'one in which women's experiences and ways of knowing are brought to the fore, not suppressed' (498). Subsequently, scholarship began to place more emphasis on empirical studies that began by examining the lives of girls in an attempt to develop theoretical explanations for girls' delinquency. These studies attempted to focus on women's experiences and the social forces that shape women's lives and experiences. However, studies attempting to understand the contexts of girls' offending by starting with an examination of their lives continue to posit gender as the primary organizing factor in girls' daily actions. Once again, the result is neglecting considerations of how race/ethnicity, class, and gender hierarchies operate as structures/systems that *simultaneously* affect the girls' lives.

One paradigm that emerged from feminist efforts to put girls' lives front and center was victimization theory. These studies attempt to link girls' delinquency to physical or sexual abuse in their lives (Browne & Finkelhor 1986; Dorne 2002; McCormack, Janus & Burgess 1986; Pereda et al. 2009; Widom 2000). Some of these studies are problematic in that they infer a causal link between abuse and delinquency, thus failing to recognize that the forces that shape the abuse are intertwined with the forces that shape delinquency or contact with the system, and are not the actual causal factors. Abuse is part of a larger structural context of the unequal distribution of resources, power, and status. Sexual abuse is a way of asserting power from a sense of feeling powerless. Just as their being at the bottom of the hierarchical structure shapes the girls' sense of self, the family/family members' sense of self and well-being is similarly shaped. Some studies have suggested that girls' delinquency or contact with the juvenile justice system evolves from criminalization of girls' attempts to escape victimization, such as abusive homes. However, this aspect of victimization theory is still problematic in that, similar to previous theories, it theorizes gender as a primary factor of social relations. Aspects of both Liberation and Victimization Theories are prevalent in many current studies that attempt to examine girls' delinquency by starting with an examination of girls' lives.

Scholarship attempting to move beyond viewing gender as a primary dichotomously constructed organizing factor attempts to understand how class (and to a lesser extent race) intersects with gender through incorporating neighborhood economic conditions as a factor in delinquency (Campbell 1990; Fishman 1995; Harper & Robinson 1999; Joe & Chesney-Lind 1995; Lauderback, Hansen, Waldorf 1992; Miller 2001, 2008; Moore 1991). However, many of these studies do not elaborate on the processes by which neighborhood social conditions intersect with gender in fostering girls' delinquency or girls' contact with the juvenile justice system. They do not theorize how gender oppression intersects with race and class oppression structures in shaping perceptions and actions of girls living in impoverished neighborhoods. Similarly to gender, many scholars view race/ethnicity in narrow terms of an individual identity or characteristic rather than as a structure comprised of resources, status, and power.

A by-product of previous studies not conceptualizing how race/ethnicity, gender, and class are simultaneous, intersecting structures is the paucity of research using navigation of power and status as a primary theoretical framework. While the literature on boys and delinquency is abundant with theories of how their delinquency is connected to attaining status, this is not the case with literature on girls and delinquency. The few scholars who use attainment of status for understanding girls view status as linked to conformity or deviance to gender roles in the context of girls and violence (Fishman 1995; Jones, 2004; Ness, 2010). These perspectives are shaped by viewing gender as an individual, dichotomously constructed attribute reflecting ideals of masculinity and femininity, embodied in notions of '*doing* gender.' For example, in her study of why girls fight, Ness (2010) theorizes that 'street fighting—offers girls in inner cities…an avenue for attaining a sense of mastery, status, and self-esteem in a social setting where legal opportunities for achievement and other psychic rewards are not otherwise easily available' (8). However, ultimately, Ness reduces her argument to a 'culture of poverty' thesis by attributing the inner-city girls' actions to having different 'cultural' standards in terms of conformity or deviance to gender roles.

In essence, studies attempting to understand the contexts of girls' offending by starting with an examination of their lives continue to posit gender, race/ethnicity, and class as individual attributes and gender as the primary organizing factor of social relations. The result is neglecting considerations of how race/ethnicity, class, and gender hierarchies operate as structures that *simultaneously* affect the girls' lives. As a result, these studies struggle to illuminate the connections between structure and agency. Hence, it is still not clear how structures of marginalization are manifested in how girls navigate their everyday lives. There is a need for illumination of the recurring negotiations of girls with structural/institutional constraints.

This study expands upon previous studies by examining how gender marginalization intersects with race and class marginalization to shape the lives of girls in the juvenile justice system. Rather than viewing gender as the primary basis of social relations and race, class, gender as additive, I conceptualize each of these as operating simultaneously, comprising one overarching structure of domination. In essence, this book attempts to examine the dialectic between structure and agency by arguing that the girls' actions are shaped by their objective circumstances of being at the bottom of a societal structure comprising the hierarchical distribution of resources, status, and power. This position shapes how the girls make sense of themselves and the world around them such that many of their actions/interactions are attempts to claim a sense of power and status.

Theoretical Frameworks

Deconstructing the relationship between structure and agency in the context of simultaneous, intersecting structures of race/ethnicity, gender, and class warrants a multi-level theoretical framework. First, symbolic interaction theory (particularly the works of Goffman and Cooley) provides a useful framework for understanding how the girls make sense of their worlds and how this shapes their actions. Symbolic interaction theory is based on the premise that people act and interact based on the meanings they attribute to surrounding circumstances, self, and others. The meanings people attribute to circumstances and self comprise dominant meanings of the society in which they are embedded. All interactions (both tangible and intangible) are in some way an exchange or 'negotiation' of these dominant meanings. Further, the Looking Glass Self, which is a part of Symbolic Interaction Theory, provides a framework for understanding identity construction based on the attribution and exchange of dominant meanings. According to the Looking Glass Self, identity is shaped by a person's understanding of how she/he is perceived by others—how she/he gives meaning to others' perceptions of her. In essence, our conception of self (identity) arises from our perception of how others view and judge us, and the effect of that perceived judgment on us.

The attribution and exchange of meanings occur in a broader structural context. To this extent, placing micro processes of symbolic interaction in the larger context of macro theories drawing upon Marx, Durkheim, and Weber provides a more comprehensive understanding of the dialectic between structure and agency. Durkheim theorized that a shared belief system is what keeps the social order. Every society, institution, and so on, has a shared belief system, commonly known as values. These shared beliefs comprise the dominant meanings—or symbols—that provide the content of exchange and negotiation processes of symbolic interaction. However, as Marx pointed out, shared belief systems are not a matter of voluntary agreement and engagement; rather, he believed that a society's shared system of beliefs is shaped by the underlying distribution of resources and power. In Marx's view, belief systems are shaped through processes of power and coercion in which those who are at the top of the hierarchical distribution of resources create and reinforce systems of beliefs to rationalize and justify their position in the hierarchy. Weber added the dimension of status to Marx's notion of a hierarchical distribution. Thus, attribution and exchange of meanings through interactions, and the construction of identity, occur in the larger structural context of the hierarchical distribution of resources, power, and status. One's position in this hierarchical structure shapes how one makes sense of self (identity), others, and how one navigates the world.

In recognizing the significance of this larger structure in shaping the exchange of meanings and the construction of identity, Goffman (1959) notes the significance of impression management in a meritocratic society and how upward mobility involves the 'presentation of proper performances…through utilizing the proper symbols' (36). These presentations of self through interpersonal exchanges become the mechanisms by which parties negotiate their places in the hierarchy: they incorporate symbols (reflected by dominant societal ideals) that give the impression of their standing as citizens of worthy status. These performances are significant since 'being affirmed culturally is a crucial element of a robust sense of self' (Goffman 1959, 36).

However, social class is not the primary organizing system of social relations; rather, class operates simultaneously with other intersecting structures, such as race/ethnicity and gender. In Notes on the Management of Spoiled Identity, Goffman (1963) further elaborates upon impression management to suggest how exchanges of dominant meanings inevitably include categorizing others and the implications for those who occupy a diminished status. Goffman suggests that if a person has an attribute making him different from others and 'a less desirable kind, then he is thus reduced in our minds from a whole and usual person to a tainted, discounted one. Such an attribute is a stigma' (3–4). Having been immersed in societal institutions and interactions, the 'stigmatized' person is aware of society's beliefs about his inferiority. In essence, the stigmatized has learned the 'normal point of view' and that 'he is disqualified according to it' (80). In navigating their lives, the stigmatized utilize various impression management techniques to preserve a sense of dignity. All individuals are engaged in navigating their lives in such a way to preserve a sense of dignity through various techniques of impression management; however, this preservation of dignity takes on added significance for the stigmatized. Whether the stigmatized accepts the 'normal point of view' is irrelevant. Whether she/he accepts it or not, the 'normal point of view' (how society makes sense of her/him) inevitably shapes how the stigmatized makes sense of surrounding circumstances and how she/he navigates life. Thus, those who occupy a devalued status along hierarchies of race/ethnicity, class, gender, and so on, have a sense of themselves as being viewed through the lens of devalued status.

Thus, drawing upon symbolic interaction theory in the broader context of theories of Marx, Durkheim, and Weber, the dynamics in this book may be understood in the following way: The girls occupy a position at the bottom of intersecting race/ethnic, class, and gender hierarchies.

As such, they are deprived of resources, status, and power, and this shapes not only their life chances but how society views them as well as how they view themselves. Because the girls have a sense of their lesser value in society, this affects the way they view and feel about themselves and shapes their actions attempting to claim some sense of worth in a society that devalues them. They are attempting to establish a sense of dignity in a world where they have known incessant 'discounting' and stigmatizing. They navigate their lives in various ways to establish a sense of validation.

This analysis also draws upon Foucault to place the girls' negotiations of power and status in the context of institutional processes. According to Foucault, the molding of citizens takes place at the institutional level. Institutions enact power and reproduce citizens and citizenship through processes of attempting to impose dominant societal meanings. Reinforcing dominant societal meanings is part of broader institutional processes replicating citizens through reproducing underlying historically constituted hierarchies of resources, power, and status. One of the ways that institutions reproduce citizenship is through the *language* of citizenship and notions of what it means to be a 'good citizen.' Whether, and the extent to which, institutional members accept the institution's definitions is an important part of the reproduction of hierarchies. Every institution (including family) has a set of processes in which membership or belonging is fostered through instilling and reinforcing dominant ideals of what it means to be a valued, accepted member. The girls negotiate these ideals and the underlying hierarchies as they navigate the institutions in their lives. In essence, these chapters are about how institutions enact power through processes of attempting to impose dominant societal meanings, thus reproducing hierarchies, and how those at the bottom of hierarchical structures navigate/negotiate these processes.

Finally, most studies of girls in the juvenile justice system present a literal accounting of the girls' activities and words rather than examining action and words in relation to larger meanings. However, encoded meanings behind activities and words, not the literal representation of facts or events, provide the substance for theorizing. Thus, this book provides rich, contextual narratives, and it is through these narratives that the processes of how dominant meanings are attributed and negotiated are revealed. Narratives of the girls' lives reveal how they live, not according to a separate set of 'subculture norms,' but according to the norms of the broader society. Through revealing how the girls manage their daily lives, these findings illustrate that while 'delinquent' is seemingly their master status, these acts are a tiny fraction of the girls' lives, and their identities and lives are far more complex than the label implies.

Chapter Summaries

The following chapters illustrate the various ways that the girls attempt to gain a sense of status and power as they navigate the institutions of family, the juvenile justice system, and neighborhood gangs. Each substantive chapter ends with an extensive conclusion and discussion section placing the findings in that chapter in a larger context of significance. Chapter 2 elaborates upon the study's setting, sample population, and methodology. Chapter 3 examines how the girls navigate power and status in their families. It illustrates how the dynamics surrounding the construction of the girls' charges evolve out of control struggles in which the girls refuse to keep a child's place, and attempt to elevate their status within their families. These power struggles result in parents collaborating with justice system authorities in attempting to restore their authority in the family, thus attempting to reinforce their daughters' status as children. In examining family power struggles, Chap. 3 draws upon Goffman's (1971) framework of 'The Insanity of Place.' The findings add to the body of literature that recognizes the criminalization of behavior that constitutes attempts to navigate the pressures of multiple marginalization. The family power struggles are shaped by the larger structural context of neighborhoods that are at the bottom of the hierarchical distribution of resources, status, and power.

Chapter 4 examines how the girls navigate power and status while they are incarcerated. It explores how a lack of status in their overall lives fosters institutional dynamics in the form of 'horizontal surveillance' in which the girls draw upon dominant ideals of citizenship to police each other in group therapy sessions. It examines how therapists utilized techniques to enlist the girls in this peer surveillance. Under pressure to demonstrate acceptance of institutional ideals, the girls used these dominant ideals to police each other in competing for status in the institution's meritocratic social order. These processes illustrate how surveillance by colleagues not in positions of power contributes to reinforcing the power of governing authority, as well as intensifying hierarchies of gender and race/ethnicity.

Chapter 5 examines how the girls reintegrated into their families after they were released. After release, girls in the juvenile justice system are likely to return to the same family power struggles that contributed to their entering the system or being incarcerated. The level of family discordance is likely to have significant consequences for the quality of life of girls after they are released, thus affecting whether they are successfully able to get off of probation. This is significant since most girls are re-incarcerated not based on new offenses, but on probation violations. Periods of incarceration are unlikely to contribute to improving the family control struggles that propelled the girls into the system. Consequently, after the girls are released, these contests for control become one of the difficult challenges with which they must contend. The findings suggest that a factor making a difference was a family's willingness to compromise on their demands that their daughters occupy a 'child's status' within the family. This chapter will illustrate the character of some of these struggles after the girls are released and suggest ways or degrees in which their modification or lack of modification impacts the girls' chances of successfully exiting the system.

Since family conflict and a sense of alienation in the family make the girls vulnerable to gaining a sense of worth through gangs, Chap. 6 examines how the girls navigated power and status in their gang associations. More specifically, this chapter examines how the girls' gang involvement is an attempt to claim a sense of status through distancing themselves from the devalued status of racial/ethnic minority women. They glorify their associations as being one of the chosen ones or chosen few. It also examines various modes of incorporation in the girls' gang associations and the consequences these have for shaping the girls' sense of self and how they navigate power and status. In essence, by using dominant ideals of citizenship to distance themselves from their devalued status, the girls are reproducing the structure of inequality. Chapter 6 concludes with considering the question 'given that the girls' actions may be seen as attempts to gain status, what are the implications for programs and policies designed to address the phenomenon of girls in the juvenile justice system?'

Finally, Chap. 7 places the books' findings in a larger historical context of the misinterpretation of the 'culture of poverty thesis' to clarify the broader relationship between hierarchical structures and dominant ideals. Understanding this relationship is critical to understanding the foundations for changing hierarchies in all institutions.

References

Adler, F. 1975. *Sisters in Crime: The Rise of the New Female Criminal*. New York: McGraw Hill.

Browne, Angela, and David Finkelhor. 1986. Impact of Child Sexual Abuse: A Review of the Research. *Psychological Bulletin* 99(1): 66–77.

Campbell, Anne. 1990. Female Participation in Gangs. In *Gangs in America*, ed. G.R. Huff. Newbury Park, CA: Sage.

Chesney-Lind, Meda. 1989. Girls' Crime and Woman's Place: Toward a Feminist Model of Female Delinquency. *Crime and Delinquency* 35: 5–29.

———. 1997. *The Female Offender: Girls, Women and Crime*. Thousand Oaks, CA: Sage.

———. 1999. Challenging Girls' Invisibility in Juvenile Court. *The Annals of The American Academy of Political and Social Sciences* 564: 185–202.

Cullen, F.T., K.M. Golden, and J.B. Cullen. 1979. Sex and Delinquency: A Partial Test of the Masculinity Hypothesis. *Criminology* 17(3): 301.

Daly, Kathleen, and Meda Chesney-Lind. 1988. Feminism and Criminology. *Justice Quarterly.* 5(4): 497–538.

Dorne, Clifford K. 2002. *An Introduction to Child Maltreatment in the United States: History, Public Policy and Research*. New York: Criminal Justice Press/ Willow Tree Press.

Fishman, L. T. 1995. The Vice Queens: An Ethnographic Study of Black Female Gang Behavior. In *The Modern Gang Reader*, ed. M. Klein, C. Maxson, and J. Miller. Los Angeles: Roxbury.

Goffman, Erving N. 1959. *The Presentation of Self in Everyday Life*. New York: Doubleday.

Goffman, Erving N 1963. *Notes on the Management of Spoiled Identity*. New York: Simon and Schuster.

Goffman, Erving N. 1971. The Insanity of Place. In *Relations in Public*, ed. Erving Goffman. New York: Harper & Row.

Harper, G., and L. Robinson. 1999. Pathways to Risk Among Inner-City African-American Adolescent Females: The Influence of Gang Membership. *American Journal of Community Psychology* 27: 383–404.

Joe, K., and M. Chesney-Lind. 1995. 'Just Every Mother's Angel' An Analysis of Gender and Ethnic Variations in Youth Gang Membership. *Gender & Society* 9: 408–431.

Jones, N. 2004. 'It's Not Where You Live, It's How You Live': How Young Women Negotiate Conflict and Violence in the Inner City. In *ANNALS of the American Academy of Political and Social Science*, ed. E. Anderson et al., 595. Thousand Oaks, CA: Sage.

Lauderback, D., J. Hansen, and D. Waldorf. 1992. Sisters Are Doin' It for Themselves: A Black Female Gang in San Francisco. *The Gang Journal* 1: 57–72.

Loy, P., and S. Norland. 1981. Gender Convergence and Delinquency. *The Sociological Quarterly* 22: 275.

McCormack, A., M. Janus, and A. Burgess. 1986. Runaway Youths and Sexual Victimization: Gender Differences in an Adolescent Runaway Population. *Child Abuse and Neglect* 10: 387–395.

Miller, Jody. 2001. *One of the Guys: Girls, Gangs, and Gender*. New York: Oxford University Press.

———. 2008. *Getting Played: African American Girls, Urban Inequality and Gendered Violence*. New York: New York University Press.

Moore, J.W. 1991. *Going Down to the Barrio: Homeboys and Homegirls in Change*. Philadelphia: Temple University Press.

Morris, R. 1964. Female Delinquency and Relational Problems. *Social Forces* 43: 82.

Morris, R 1965. Attitudes Toward Delinquency by Delinquents, Non-Delinquents and Their Friends. *British Journal of Criminology* 5: 249.

Ness, Cindy. 2010. *Why Girls Fight: Female Youth Violence in the Inner City*. New York: The New York University Press.

Pereda, N., et al. 2009. The Prevalence of Child Sexual Abuse in Community and Student Samples: A Meta-Analysis. *Clinical Psychology Review* 29(4): 328–338.

Thornton, William E. and Jennifer James. 1979. Masculinity And Delinquency Revisited. *The British Journal of Criminology.* 19(3): 225–241.

Widom, C.S. 1979. Female Offenders: Three Assumptions about Self-Esteem Sex Role Identity and Feminism. *Criminal Justice and Behaviour* 6(5): 365.

Widom, C.S 2000. Childhood Victimization: Early Adversity, Later Psychopathology. *National Institute of Justice Journal* 242: 3–9.

2

Getting into Place/Gaining Acceptance and Trust

Research Setting

This study is based on ethnographic research I conducted at a co-ed county juvenile justice institution in a large city. Although this institution was a lockdown facility consisting of 60 residents, it attempted to encompass group home living by dividing the residents into bungalows comprising groups of 10. This is one of a handful of institutions to which youth may be sentenced after spending time in juvenile hall and being charged with a minor offense. However, this was the only lockdown institution that included therapeutic practices as part of the rehabilitation program. Although the institution is co-ed, the girls and boys are kept separate from each other with the exception of time spent in the classroom and time spent during recreational activities. The only gender-integrated sphere within this institution was the school, where the residents attended regularly scheduled classes in working toward high school graduation. Although there was a school on the premises, the school seemed to be peripheral to the institution's merit program. Neither school nor education is mentioned in any of the expectations

© The Author(s) 2017
C.P. Davis, *Girls and Juvenile Justice*,
DOI 10.1007/978-3-319-42845-1_2

at each of the levels of the tiered merit-ladder system, and actions that occurred in school were not considered in the evaluation system calculating daily points for each girl.

In speaking with staff, I learned that the underlying premise guiding whether youths are sent here versus a regular lockdown facility is that the youths sent to this institution are deemed by the judge to be 'not bad kids' but rather kids who had bad circumstances in their lives, such as 'family problems.' This discretionary sorting of bad kids from 'wayward' kids reflects the ongoing historical processes of the juvenile justice system's attempt from its initiation to separate and make distinctions between categories of children: 'wayward' and 'neglected' children from 'criminal' children (Feld 1999). In the evolution of the juvenile justice system, this tension between wayward and criminal embodies the tension between treatment and punishment. Wayward children were seen as a product of circumstances that had not instilled them with appropriate moral values; consequently, wayward children were seen as amenable to treatment that involved instilling appropriate values. However, the lines between treatment and punishment are blurred. The blurred lines between punishment and treatment are reflected in the historical development of the rise of therapeutic interventions in penal institutions.

The mission of the institution is to provide a therapeutic-based program of rehabilitation to youths; thus, one of the organizing structures of the institution was required daily group therapy sessions held in each bungalow, plus weekly family group therapy sessions. There were ten girls in each bungalow, and therefore ten girls in each group therapy session. This institution did not use a formal therapeutic model. Rather, one of the supervisors/therapists formulated the approach by saying that these youths were not capable of real therapy; instead, the goal was to get them to communicate. This institution refers to participation in group therapy as 'working,' and the labor in these sessions may be viewed as consisting of the production of a new (moral) self, thus illustrating worthiness of citizenship. While the formal organizing system reinforced obedience, following rules, harmonious relationships, and distributed rewards accordingly, the heart of the formal organizing system took place within the sphere of group therapy.

The underlying merit-based system provided the ideals and incentives for the defining and ranking of self and others in the hierarchical structure. This merit system reinforced institutional ideals through horizontal surveillance. This organizing structure was a five-tiered level system ranging from Introduction Level to Level four, with Level Four indicating the highest level of progress and designated by the institution as the level of 'citizenship.' The institution's merit system reflects and reinforces ideas of individual achievement and meritocracy (exemplified by the expectations listed at each level) in the larger society outside the institution. The expectations outlined at each level reflect meritocratic goals, such as acceptance of personal responsibility and individual agency. Level four (designated by the institution as the level of citizenship) represents the pinnacle of success, and at that level, the residents are expected to have mastered the expectations, thus entitling them to the pinnacle of privileges: outings (trips outside the institution).

Privileges below level four were in the form of allowing more expression of 'self,' such as being allowed to post pictures, draw on the walls, being allowed to have grooming materials, and so on. The girls were rewarded and sanctioned through a daily point system. As long as each girl did each activity with no 'disruptions,' she received the maximum number of points for that activity, so that at the end of each day, she received a score for the day and each daily score was added for a weekly score and this weekly score determined the girls' place on the merit ladder. The duration of the institution's program is approximately nine months. Around the point nearing nine months of a girl's stay, a release hearing is held in which the girl's probation officer (who is also her therapist) goes before the judge to give a progress report and make a release recommendation.

The number of points a girl accumulated each day determined her position in the institution's level system. This distribution of points may be viewed as analogous to the distribution of wages (or similar resources) in the broader society. The number of points corresponds to one's position in the institution's merit system, just as one's income generally corresponds to one's position in the socio-economic system in the broader society. Just as failure to produce a product on the outside may result in failure to be paid, failure to produce the required aspects of self in the institution results in failure to accumulate merit points.

Just as resources affect how people navigate their lives in the broader society, the distribution of points determines even the smallest details of the girls' daily routines/lives. Even the simplest functions, such as getting up in the morning, are determined by the distribution of points:

> I asked the girls about getting up in the morning and they explained to me that it is done by the point system and that the person with the highest points had to get up first, while the person with the least points got to sleep later and was the last to be awakened. Helen explained to me that this was really not as it seemed because although she got to sleep the latest, it meant she had the least time to get ready in the morning, depending on how much time everybody before her took, she might barely have time to get dressed and get out the door to school.

Time is the reward afforded by accumulating the requisite points, more specifically, time to get ready in the morning, which provides opportunities to access other opportunities, such as utilizing the bathroom first. The resources (points) are distributed such that the person at the bottom of the level system has less resources (time to prepare, clean bathroom, time to eat breakfast, etc.) In essence, similarly to the hierarchical structure on the outside of the institution, the person at the bottom lacks the resources to comfortably navigate even the smallest of details of her daily existence. While these 'getting up' privileges are shaped by the institution's point system/privilege ladder, these structures in turn are shaped by the structures and ideologies in the broader society that emphasize and reinforce the protestant work ethic and the alleged benefits of rising early. As noted in the above scenario, the amount of resources allotted to each girl in her morning routine depended upon how many resources the girls above her utilized, thus reinforcing competition for resources. For this population, both inside and outside, competitions mirror each other in that in both instances, there are no real rewards; rather, they are competing for access to basic human dignities and rights.

Sample Population

The data on which this book is based consist of field notes from two years of participant-observations of 50 girls, periodic taped interviews with 30 of those girls during incarceration, and field notes and interviews with 7 of the 30 after they were released from incarceration. The ethnic composition of the girls was predominately African-American and Latina (Salvadoran and Mexican), and they were from predominately under-privileged to lower/working class neighborhoods. Of the 30 girls periodically interviewed, 15 were Latina, 14 were African-American, and 1 was Anglo. At the time I began the research, all of the girls were incarcerated in a co-ed public detention facility for minor offenders between the ages of 13 and 18.

Of the 30 girls interviewed, the following charges were represented (the total number of charges is greater than 30 because each girl had multiple charges): 21 had violation of probation charges (including violating curfew, dirty drug tests, and missing court dates); 17 had assault charges (including assault and battery, and assault with a deadly weapon); 7 had prostitution charges; 7 had grand theft auto charges; 5 had shoplifting charges; 4 had possession of drug charges (2 of them had possession and sales charges); 4 had terrorist threat charges; 2 had vandalism/destruction of property charges; and 2 had charges of receiving stolen property. Many of these girls had been in and out of the system and spent time in other institutions. Cycling in and out of institutions is a common phenomenon in the juvenile justice system.

Of my sample interview population of 30 girls, 57 percent had family/guardian conflicts that facilitated contact with the system (13 percent), movement toward detention and incarceration (34 percent), or both contact and movement (10 percent). Of the remaining 43 percent, 17 percent were girls who did not have families and came into the system from the Department of Child and Family Services (DCFS). Girls from DCFS often move into the juvenile justice system as a result of the same types of control struggles that are faced by girls coming from families. Just as the standoff between girls and their parents often results in the parents' reliance on the justice system to help them establish authority over the actions of their daughters, the standoff between girls and foster parents or group home staff often results in foster parents' or staff reliance on the system to help them establish authority.

Of those girls who did not come into the system from the DCFS, the majority lived with their mothers and stepfathers. The remaining were almost evenly divided between girls living with grandparents, girls living in two-parent homes, and girls living in single-mother homes. For simplification, I will use the term 'parent' in the sense of adult guardian. The actual person may be a grandmother or other relative. For the most part, even in families that included either men parents or guardians, maintaining authority with the girls was primarily left to the woman parent or guardian.

Gaining Access

After meeting with the facility's clinical director and clinical staff, I gained access to this facility through a juvenile court order granting me permission to do a participant-observation and interview study of all activities of the girls at the facility. Although I did not have a specific question guiding my research, I was interested in how the girls navigated the institution's rehabilitation program, which is a merit-based system. Before entering, I had some vague plan of dividing time between staff (bungalow supervisors, clinical, and probation) and girls; upon entering, I decided that I would spend all of my time in the bungalows with the girls. When I made this decision, I had no ideas of trying to distance myself from the staff in order to gain the girls' trust—I made the decision because that was where all the action was and it was simply more interesting than staff meetings, and so on. However, months later, I realized this decision may have had some significance in gaining some degree of trust and acceptance from both the girls and the bungalow staff when in a hushed conversation between bungalow staff and one of the girls about the bungalow supervisor, one of the girls motioned that I was listening to the conversation and the bungalow staff said 'Carla doesn't spend any time up there with them—she's okay.'

There was much less social distance between bungalow staff and the girls than between higher-level staff and the girls, so associating with bungalow staff was not as much of an issue in gaining the girls' trust. Additionally, eating dinner with the girls seemed to somehow help in gaining acceptance and establishing rapport. I ate dinner regularly with the girls and alternated between the two bungalows. Before long, it became customary for the girls who were setting up for dinner to ask me whether I was eating with them that day so that they could set a place for me at the table. At one point, one of the girls said to me, 'That's what I like about you—you eat county food.'

Although I never spent any time with higher-level staff, I could not have spent all of my time 'hanging out' with the girls if the clinical director and bungalow supervisors (clinical staff) had any objections or reservations to my doing so. They placed no limitations on my comings and goings and were willing to let me come and go, sit, watch, and listen whenever I chose. Their generosity was in part because at least a couple of them felt that I would in some way be a positive role model for the girls, that is, it would be good for girls of color to be around a woman of color who had graduated from college. I chose my first bungalow because the bungalow supervisor was so immediately willing to let me spend time hanging out in the bungalow and told me that I was welcome to spend time with the girls anytime.

I initially introduced myself to the girls and the bungalow staff person in one of their group therapy sessions, which was led by the bungalow supervisor. I told them that I wanted to write a paper on how they were adjusting to the institution and that I wanted to hang out with them in the bungalow to see how they lived there and how they interacted with the staff and each other. I gave each of the girls a consent form that explained the study, the nature and extent of my observations, that is, what I was observing, and so on, and the nature and extent of the interviews (I was careful to write it in language they could understand). I emphasized that I was not affiliated with staff and that I would not tell staff anything they said or did (unless they said or did something to harm themselves or others, or if I learned someone was harming them). One of the girls asked me if I would tell staff if I learned that one of them was going to AWOL, and I shook my head no, this was something that I was not obliged to tell. The bungalow supervisor then said, 'Of course the smart thing to do if you're going to AWOL is to keep it to yourself.' In the following days, the girls began giving me their signed consent forms.

Since the bungalow supervisor of my first bungalow was an Anglo man, after a couple of months, I decided upon another bungalow because I wanted to see whether there were different dynamics in a bungalow with an African-American woman as bungalow supervisor. This bungalow supervisor initially wanted to know more about my research plan, then, after hearing that I had been observing in one of the other bungalows, gave her consent. Once she gave her consent, she also did not place any limitations on my comings, goings, and observations. I spent most of my time literally sitting in the bungalows, observing and talking to the girls while they went about their daily business. In the beginning, I did not go out of my way to try to get to know them or to ask them questions. After a while, the girls became accustomed to my being there, and conversations between the girls and me became more frequent.

In the beginning, I repeatedly had to distinguish my role as researcher from that of counselor/therapist, as some of the girls seemed to think that I was in the bungalow to listen to their problems and provide emotional support. Sometimes as soon as I arrived, I would be greeted by one of the girls with 'Can I talk to you?' While I wanted to hear what was on their minds, I was careful not to misrepresent myself as a counselor and to make sure the girls understood that when we talked it would not be for the purpose of counseling or providing advice. I had anticipated this dilemma ahead of time because the clinical director had warned me that this would probably happen and that I should be prepared to deal with it. He had told me that the girls were extremely 'emotionally needy' and would want to talk to me about their problems.

Methodology

Participant-Observations

My 'Chicago School' method for gathering data and my Symbolic Interaction theoretical framework for analyzing data go hand in hand in attempting to understand the perceptions and actions of the girls.

In essence, both rely on the assumption that in order to understand people's actions, it is imperative to be able to see things through their eyes. To collect rich data on how the girls made sense of their lives, I conducted participant-observations. The underlying logic of participant-observations is that simple observation is not sufficient for ascertaining the viewpoints of others; rather, seeing things from the viewpoint of others requires participation in their daily routines. I participated in daily activities with the girls in two of the bungalows and observed their interactions (in their bungalows, during recreational activities, at breakfast/lunch/dinner, etc.) for approximately five to six hours a day, at least four days a week, at varying times, for a period of two years. This enabled me to interact with the girls, as well as to study institutional processes.

The method of participant-observation is particularly useful for examining the connections between structure and agency, as well as for examining processes of power manifested in institutional dynamics. It provides a way to gain access to the everyday conversations and narratives that provide the substance for analyzing the ideological and material imperatives that provide clues to the connection between structure and agency. Observations were recorded in written field notes at the end of each observation day. I never took notes while I was observing because I feel this is a sure way to remind those whom you are observing that you view them first and foremost as research subjects.

Interviews

I did not ask the girls any questions about aspects of their lives, either in conversations or in interviews, until after I had known them for several weeks and they had become accustomed to my presence. I was keenly aware of the power embedded in asking personal questions, particularly in asking marginalized populations questions about their lives. The interviews occurred after months of having established rapport by 'hanging out' with the girls. Some justification is necessary for using qualitative interviews with the girls to track their career paths in the juvenile justice system. Court records do not reveal the contexts and circumstances of offenses, making it nearly impossible to unveil the significance of family dynamics such as those revealed in this study. Of the 50 girls included in the participant-observations, I conducted at least two audiotaped interviews (and many more for several of the girls) of each of 30 girls while they were incarcerated. The remaining 20 left before I had a chance to interview them.

The interviews were continuous and unstructured (in the form of conversations) and primarily consisted of the girls telling me about their lives before and after they entered the system. Through these interviews, I collected data on their lives and activities leading up to entering the system and incarceration, as well as their experiences during incarceration. While I did not formally interview their parents, I was able to substantiate many of the girls' accounts through informal conversations with parents, probation officers, as well as by sitting in on family group therapy sessions. Of these 30 girls, I conducted interviews of 7 girls at various points after they were released, collecting data on their post-release experiences, with particular emphasis on how they reintegrated into family relationships.

Getting the Girls to Talk in the Interviews

Hanging out with the girls in the bungalows and letting them get a sense of me in the weeks before the interviews helped in getting them to open up and talk more freely in the interviews. Before I began conducting the interviews, I did not have a clear idea of how they would take place, or how much the girls would disclose, and so on. I saw the interviews as being of secondary importance to the observations and thought they would just be a matter of my running a down a list of questions and the girls giving their short responses. However, after I conducted the first interview (actually, during the first interview), I realized that the interview data were going to be much more powerful than I had realized. This was so because in all of the literature that I had read on girls in the juvenile justice system, none of them had given me such insight and such a feel for what their day-to-day lives were really like—how they actually spent their time on the outside, away from home. I asked very few questions during the interviews and basically asked the girls to tell me what were the events leading up to them getting into the system and then once they were in the system, how they got from point A to point B, and so on. The girls provided rich narratives of their lives.

Basically, I presented the interview process to the girls by telling them that I wanted to know about their lives before they came to this institution. While I told the girls that I wanted to know how they got into the system and traveled through the system, underneath this, I was fascinated with the fact that although these girls were technically children, they had faced more challenges than most grown women face in a lifetime. I was interested in knowing how they did it—what were the struggles they faced and how they navigated these struggles. I wanted to know how they navigated chaotic existences where there were constant obstacles and barely a chance to recover before the next obstacle presented itself.

For the girls, only a couple of them seemed to fully understand my role as a researcher (interestingly, the two that understood this role and the concept of research were the two who most readily let their barriers down and shared their lives). It was only toward the end of my research that I gained an understanding of how most of the other girls viewed the interviews. One evening, one of the girls and I excused ourselves early from a special dinner that was hosted by an outside group so that I could interview her. As we were leaving and saying our goodbyes, the girl announced 'she's going to interview me,' and one of the other girls said 'oh—you're going to love it—she makes you feel so special—like you're really important and you're being interviewed for television' and a few other girls chimed in agreeing. These girls are, after all, part of the MTV generation and, to them, interviews have special significance, that is, when you are being interviewed, it means you are important and/or interesting.

Many of the girls vaguely had a notion that I was writing some sort of paper or a book or some sort of articles or doing some sort of documentary or doing some sort of expose about their lives. For the most part, they were not quite sure what it was, but they wanted to be a part of it. It was also a welcome distraction that served the purpose of giving them time away from the bungalow and a break from their daily routines. In other words, for the most part, they did not have anything better to do with their time. The only area in which I sensed at times some of the girls were holding back was when I asked them about their gang associations.

Although the girls never refused to talk about anything gang related, I sometimes sensed that some of the girls gave the least possible information about time spent with their gangs.

Problems with Follow-Up after Release

The most difficult part of the research was keeping in touch with the girls after they were released so that I could follow their lives on the outside. Whereas while incarcerated they may not have had anything better to do with their time than engage in interviews, once on the outside, they had plenty of other things vying for their time. I was only able to keep up with seven girls after release and of these seven only two remained devoted to doing the interviews on a regular basis. Not surprisingly, these were the two who had the most positive progress after the release. I felt that some of the girls once they were released were afraid or hesitant to let me know if they thought they were not doing well on the outs. I now realize that it is not productive to present post-release research as 'I want to interview you after you leave to see how you do on the outside.' This statement implies that I will somehow be judging and measuring whether they are doing 'well,' which may make those who think they are not doing 'well' reluctant to participate in the interviews after they are released. Additionally, time constraints prohibited my more vigilantly tracking the girls after they were released from incarceration. This resulted in a small sample size of seven, from which it is difficult to definitively draw out emerging patterns of post-release adjustment.

Data Analysis

I used grounded theory methods to conduct an inductive analysis of the interview and fieldnote data to discover the patterns that provide the basis for the book's primary argument. Grounded theory consists of a set of inductive strategies for discovering patterns and meanings in large masses of disorganized information. Grounded theory methods involves analyzing processes in data by looking at words and actions in relation to meaning, thus avoiding static analyses that merely provide a literal accounting of words and actions. Rather than viewing data through preconceived categories, new ways of representing and understanding reality are revealed through the analytical process of integrating and assimilating data inductively (Charmaz 1983, 1990; Strauss, Anselm, Corbin 1990, 1997). In contrast to studies analyzing data through preconceived categories of preliminary literature reviews, I conducted my literature review after identifying emerging salient themes in the data. This is consistent with the purpose of grounded theory methods. This process involved multiple stages of 'mining' the data (coding), with each stage becoming more conceptual in terms of linking the words and actions to larger ideas of meaning. In sifting through the data, I made comparisons between girls and comparisons of data from the same girls at different points in time. Through these processes, I began to see the patterns and relationships in the data that served as the basis for developing my analytic framework and, ultimately, my argument.

Data Presentation

Rich qualitative research reveals processes rather than frequencies; thus, rather than revealing across several girls, the presentation of data focuses on a few to illuminate larger patterns found in the data. Rich contextual narratives provide the data necessary for revealing processes of how dominant meanings are attributed and negotiated. Because grounded theory involves extracting layers of meanings embedded in the data, this necessitates incorporating substantive passages in the presentation of data. Thus, this book leads with the data and places the girls' narratives front and center. Both interview and fieldnote passages are presented. Passages from interviews are distinguished by the pseudonyms of the participants. All other passages are excerpts from fieldnotes. While I tried to present as much of the data as possible to preserve the richness of context, space limitations dictate shortening many of the passages. Thus, areas where I cut parts of the narratives are distinguished by ellipses: '...'

References

Charmaz, Kathy. 1983. The Grounded Theory Method: An Explication and Interpretation. In *Contemporary Field Research: A Collection of Readings*, ed. R.M. Emerson, 109–126. Boston: Little, Brown.

———. 1990. 'Discovering' Chronic Illness: Using Grounded Theory. *Social Science & Medicine* 30: 1161–1172.

Feld, Barry. 1999. *Bad Kids: Race and the Transformation of the Juvenile Court.* New York: Oxford University Press.

Strauss, Anselm, and Juliet Corbin. 1990. *Basics of Qualitative Research: Grounded Theory Procedures and Techniques*. Newbury Park, CA: Sage.

———. 1997. *Grounded Theory in Practice*. Thousand Oaks, CA: Sage.

3

Getting Into the System: Negotiating Power and Status in the Family

MARA: She [grandmother] can watch a movie and she'll be happy with me—if I say 'I love you,' she'll be happy with me, if she gets a bill in the mail, she'll be pissed off for the rest of the week…she'll be like, 'I'm *tired* of this *fucking* place and I don't wanna *be* here.'

Studies of families of girls in the juvenile justice system have generally used a functionalist perspective and neglected consideration of families as a site of navigation of power and status. However, understanding processes of negotiation of power and status in families is critical to understanding families as a whole, as well as the construction of identity of individual family members. Social and economic marginalization fractures family relationships by impacting the distribution of resources, power, and status within families. Conflicts occur within families at all social locations in the hierarchical structure; however, occupying a position at the bottom of the hierarchical structure poses added pressures that exacerbate potentials for conflict. One way that marginalization strains family relationships is that it weakens the foundation for parental authority. Parental authority as well as family solidarity relies on the unequal distribution of power

© The Author(s) 2017
C.P. Davis, *Girls and Juvenile Justice*,
DOI 10.1007/978-3-319-42845-1_3

and status in the parent–child relationship. Through examining the contexts of the girls' offenses, family conflict over issues of parental authority emerged as a salient factor underlying the girls' initial contact with the system and the construction of their recorded offenses. The findings in this chapter add to the body of literature noting the criminalization of girls' attempts to navigate the pressures of multiple marginalization.

Although the girls are technically children, the girls' lives are not the lives of children in that they are exposed to and navigate circumstances that are not usually encountered until adulthood. Actually, the girls navigate circumstances that most adults never encounter. Social and economic strains make it difficult to have a child's life. It is this context that shapes the girls' sense of self such that they may not make sense of themselves as being children. Just as the girls have not been able to live a child's life, social and economic strains have made it difficult for parents to fulfill the dominant ideal of parents as providers, protectors, and nurturers. These processes contribute to the girls' invalidating parental authority. In these control struggles, the girls refuse to keep a child's place and attempt to elevate their status within their families while parents (or grandparents) attempt to assert their authority. These power struggles result in parents collaborating with justice system authorities in an attempt to restore their authority in the family, thus reinforcing their daughters' status as children. These findings suggest the continuing significance of status offenses in the arrest and incarceration of girls.

Before the 1974 Juvenile Justice and Delinquency Prevention Act, girls were arrested or detained primarily for status offenses (offenses that would not be regarded as wrongdoing if committed by someone 18 or older). Although decriminalization of status offenses should have resulted in a diminished presence of girls in the justice system, there has instead been an increase. From arrests to detention, the proportion of girls in the juvenile justice system has increased at every stage of the process over the last 20 years (Balck and Sherman, Gender Injustice Report 2015). There was nearly a 50 percent increase in the arrest of girls between 1992 and 2012: while in 1992, girls made up 20 percent of the children arrested in the USA, by 2012, they accounted for 29 percent of children arrested (Balck and Sherman 2015; Puzzanchera: OJJDP Report 2014). In 2013, nearly 40 percent of detained girls were incarcerated for status offenses or technical violations (Puzzanchera: OJJDP Report 2014; Sickmund et al.: OJJDP Report 2013a, 2013b). African-American girls are the fastest growing segment of the population, and in 2013 were 20 percent more likely to be detained than Anglo girls, while Native American girls were 50 percent more likely to be detained (Balck and Sherman 2015; Puzzanchera and Hockenberry 2014). Some reports have suggested that a possible reason for the increase is aggressive efforts by police when intervening in domestic violence incidents (Balck and Sherman 2015). Within this context, one possibility is that challenges to parental authority are being constructed and processed under other 'official' categories of crimes or delinquencies. Thus, examining the ways that family power struggles may result in the arrest of girls remains critical. Through ethnographic fieldwork and interviews, this chapter reveals some of the negotiations and practices of parents and the juvenile justice system post deinstitutionalization of status offenses.

Getting into the System: Status Offenses and the Gendered Double Standard

Previous literature documents how girls in the juvenile justice system have historically been disproportionately sanctioned for status offenses (Belknap and Holsinger 1998; Chesney-Lind and Shelden 2004; Cohn 1970; Datesman et al. 1975; Gibbons and Griswold 1957; Odem 1995; Odem and Schlossman 1991; Schlossman and Wallach 1978). The phenomenon of girls entering the system through status offenses is part of the broader historical development of the creation of organizations to monitor the social and moral behavior of 'troubled' youths who do not commit serious offenses. This evolution led to the establishment of the first juvenile court in 1899. In essence, the purpose was to distinguish delinquent from criminal behavior (Platt 1969).

In the nineteenth century, with the growth of urbanization, industrialization, immigration, and increased geographic mobility, communal mechanisms of social control collapsed. An underclass emerged, labeled as poor, who were perceived as living in 'slum' environments regarded as unregulated and lacking in social rules (Platt 1969). Children of the poor were primary among those whom it was believed could benefit from rehabilitation. Most were recent immigrants, with ethnic backgrounds different from that of established American residents. In general, these children were not considered hardened offenders, but instead were considered to be vagrant or wayward youths whose non-criminal behavior could be rehabilitated. They were often thought of as 'incorrigible' or 'beyond control,' and considered to be living in environments likely to foster delinquency and criminality (Chesney-Lind and Shelden 2004). Social reformers emphasized the temporary and reversible nature of adolescent crime and believed that 'delinquent' children must be 'saved' by preventing them from pursuing criminal careers. Institutions proliferated to reform the behaviors of these youths. This 'child saving' movement crafted a system of government that had unprecedented authority to intervene in the lives of families, particularly in the lives of youths (Empey 1982; Platt 1969; Zatz 1982).

The moral behavior of girls was of specific concern to the 'child savers' (Belknap and Holsinger 1998; Chesney-Lind and Shelden 2004). As part of this reform movement, White middle class women reformers sought to protect White working class girls from straying from moral paths. These middle class women's activities revolved around monitoring the moral and sexual behaviors of the working class, particularly immigrant girls (Chesney-Lind and Shelden 2004; Gordon 1988; Odem 1995). Based upon middle class ideals of female sexual propriety, reformers assumed they had the authority to define what was 'appropriate' behavior for working class women and girls. Girls who did not conform to these ideals were labeled as 'wayward' and deemed to be in need of control by the state in the form of juvenile courts, reformatories, and 'training schools' (Chesney-Lind and Shelden 2004; Odem 1995). Black female 'delinquents' were placed in adult institutions or sent out of State until it became practically or fiscally unfeasible to do so (Young 1994). Research examining court practices after the court's initial inception reveal a preoccupation with girls' sexuality, as revealed in charges relating to some form of 'waywardness' or 'immorality,' and view contemporary status-type offense charges as buffer charges for suspected sexual activity/misconduct (Chesney-Lind and Shelden 2004; Odem 1995; Odem and Schlossman 1991; Schlossman and Wallach 1978; Shelden 1981).

Studies also document the historical pattern of parental use of the status offense category in referring their daughters to authorities for a variety of activities (Andrews and Cohn 1974; Belknap and Holsinger 1998; Chesney-Lind and Shelden 2004; Odem and Schlossman 1991; Teitelbaum and Gough 1977). This coupled with the vagueness of status offense statutes and the precedence of authorities and courts to uphold parental authority make the misuse of the status offense category particularly likely (Sussman 1977). The recognition that some parents turn to the courts to enforce their authority is thought to be a primary reason for many girls' presence in the juvenile justice system (Chesney-Lind and Shelden 2004).

After establishment of the juvenile court, the next major attempt to address non-criminal 'troubled' youth was in the 1960s when another reform movement attempted to redefine categorization of wayward/non-criminal offenders (Empey 1973, Zatz 1982). The result of these reform efforts was the 1974 Juvenile Justice and Delinquency Prevention Act. The federal government recognized a specific category of offenders—'status offenders'—and ordered measures that would remove or divert this group of juveniles away from the juvenile justice system and away from incarceration. Since historically girls have been disproportionately sanctioned for status offenses, the immediate impact of the 1974 Juvenile Justice and Delinquency Act was greater for girls. Girls' institutionalization rates for status offenses fell by 44 percent (Chesney-Lind 1989; Krisberg and Schwartz 1983). However, this decline in the institutionalization of status offenders leveled off between 1979 and 1982 and there is continuing concern that status offenders are not being sufficiently differentiated from 'delinquents' and that they are still largely represented in the justice system (Arthur D. Little Inc. 1977, Balck and Sherman, Gender Injustice Report 2015; Chesney-Lind and Shelden 2004; Chesney-Lind and Shelden 1998; Federle and Chesney-Lind 1992; Schwartz et al. 1984; Zatz 1982).

Previous literature suggests two opposing views for the impact of deinstitutionalization on the discretionary powers of the police, with some asserting that it has increased discretionary powers, allowing circumvention of the 1974 Juvenile Justice and Delinquency Prevention Act (Klein 1979; Lemert 1981; Austin and Krisberg 1981), and others arguing that deinstitutionalization has weakened the discretionary powers of the police (Schwartz 1989). Previous literature has suggested that status-type offenses are being relabeled as criminal offenses (Mahoney and Fenster 1982; Klein 1979) and that some actions constituting non-serious family conflicts have been relabeled upward as violent or assault charges (Mayer 1994; Acoca 1999; Acoca and Dedel 1998; Chesney-Lind and Shelden 1998, 2004). This is thought to be one reason underlying the increase in assault charges for girls, particularly a rise in the category of 'other' assaults. This is particularly thought to be a significant factor in African-American girls' prevalence in the system (Bartollas 1993). While authorities may have historically incarcerated White, immigrant working class girls for protectionist reasons during the child-saving movement, Black and Brown girls are now the ones likely to be detained or incarcerated because, like Black and Brown boys, they are seen as dangerous, out of control, and in need of higher levels of supervision.

The findings in this chapter begin to provide evidence of the processes of relabeling status-type offenses as criminal offenses. The data illustrate how these families in their interactions with authorities have negotiated alternative methods for dealing with 'troublesome' teenage girls since laws have restrained courts from responding vigorously to status-type offenses.

Theoretical Framework: The Insanity of Place

Institutions reproduce citizens and citizenship through processes of reproducing existing hierarchies of resources, power, and status. Families are no different. Conflicts over parental authority form the basis upon which parents eventually turn to the justice system to seek help in restoring their authority with their daughters. While enforcing the gendered double standard is an underlying source of tension between parents and their daughters, this in itself does not explain how the girls come into contact with the system. Goffman's (1971) 'The Insanity of Place' provides a useful framework for understanding negotiation of power and status within families, as well as the processes by which girls come in contact with the juvenile justice system. Although Goffman's framework focuses on the family, it may be used to analyze negotiation of power and status in any institution.

In 'The Insanity of Place,' Goffman (1971) examines the processes in families by which a person comes to be classified as mentally ill and committed to hospitalization. According to Goffman, the productive functioning or welfare of a family depends upon family members supporting the expected internal order of authority relationships. In supporting the internal order of a family, members know and keep their places in the family structure. When a family member fails to support the internal order by not keeping his or her expected social position in relation to others within the family, this threatens one of the fundamental elements upon which family unity is based.

A breakdown in family solidarity begins when a family member, for whatever reason, feels the life that others in the family have been according him or her is no longer sufficient; thus the member makes demands for change. In response, other family members may accept these demands for change as valid and modify the structure of the family in accordance, or they may refuse to recognize the demands and attempt to maintain the existing social structure. It is the latter, when family members decide not to honor or recognize the family member's demands for change and the demanding family members' refusal to fall back to the status quo, that results in increasing tension. In this standoff, the family member may either voluntarily withdraw from the family organization or remain a part of the family. If he or she chooses to remain with the family, but refuses to fall back to the status quo in family relationships, the member in effect promotes himself or herself in the family hierarchy, thus beginning his or her 'manic' activity. According to Goffman, the demands of the 'maniac' are not necessarily bizarre in themselves, but are bizarre coming from the person with respect to his or her social location in the family. At this breaking point, the stronger of the two participants may form a collaborative arrangement with a third party to control the weaker party's environment and definition of the situation.

The parents (primarily mothers) act as informal agents of control by attempting to assert authority over their daughters' actions. Rather than accepting their parent(s)' authority, these girls challenge parental assertions of authority and demand the same autonomy over their actions as have the parents. Economic and social marginalization of families shapes these dynamics. The girls' promotion of themselves in the family hierarchy to that of an equal plane as their parents is disruptive to the internal organization of the family. In these instances, the parents neither physically withdraw, nor do they reconstitute the family organization to accommodate the self-assumptions of autonomy of their daughters. Instead, in attempting to restore their authority with their daughters, these parents form collaborative arrangements with the justice system to either threaten the girls into obeying parental authority or have the girls removed by detention if they do not act accordingly.

Frequently, it is the collusion of families and the justice system that places the girls in the category of delinquent. This reflects how power is exercised and reinforced through controlling the definition of a situation. This collusion is accentuated by formal social control agents' racial and ethnic stereotypes shaping perceptions of Black and Brown girls as dangerous, promiscuous, and in need of supervision. While Goffman's framework provides a base for understanding these family dynamics, an understanding of this collusion is deepened when Goffman's framework is coupled with literature (Bishop and Frazier 1992; Bridges and Steen 1998; Gaarder et al. 2004; Leiber and Stairs 1996; Miller 1994; Wordes et al. 1994) exploring how dominant ideas about racial and ethnic minorities affect perceptions and subsequent processing by formal social control agents.

As this chapter will illustrate, tensions escalate as the girls persist in their autonomous conceptions and accompanying demands/actions, while their parents exercise great efforts in attempts to bring the girls back into appropriate relationship to them: a relationship in which their daughters keep a 'child's place.' It is not so much that their daughter's actions represent delinquent acts as much as that the actions are out of line with her expected social position in the family. The remainder of this chapter examines how power and status are negotiated between the girls and their parent(s) or guardians, and how a breakdown in these negotiations may facilitate contact, entry, and movement through the juvenile justice system. Since the 1974 Deinstitutionalization Act restrained courts from responding vigorously to status-type offenses, families in their interactions with authorities have negotiated alternative methods for dealing with control struggles with teenage girls.

Negotiating Power and Status: 'Going Out'

At the root of the girls' family conflicts are struggles over control, in which the parent attempts to establish authority over the girl's actions while the girl resists this authority in an attempt to gain autonomy. Family control struggles revolve around such issues as doing chores, going to school, seeing boys, hanging out with friends, curfews, and time spent talking on the phone. However, the most contentious issue in these control struggles is the girls' desire to have the freedom to 'go out'—to spend time away from home. Negotiating 'going out' has a different level of significance in families who live in marginalized neighborhoods. The stakes are much higher for both the girls and their parents because their neighborhoods' lack of resources exposes the girls to surrounding conditions that exploit their powerlessness. Parents (or grandparents) attempt to establish authority over their daughter's freedom to 'go out,' or spend time away from home by using varying strategies to control or restrict it, while the girls use various strategies to counter these restrictive measures. If parental authority is intact, the daughters may simply abide by these restrictions. Alternatively, they may attempt to negotiate these arrangements by pleading and agreeing to be back by a certain time:

> MARA (Age 16): Going out. Wanting to go out is a big thing in my house. Cause they'll be like, 'no you don't wanna come back at this time and da-da-da-da-da.' I'll be like, 'well why don't you let me come back at ten o'clock? I'ma be here.' 'No, cause it's a school night and it's this and it's that.'

At least at this point, although Mara is challenging authority by pleading to go out, she appears to be keeping her place in the hierarchy of the family. She makes demands for change, which are denied by her grandparents and she appears to acquiesce to their position; thus parental authority appears to be intact.

Alternatively, there may be a breakdown in parental authority, and a girl may choose to ignore restrictions on going out. The mother, rather than the daughter, resorting to pleading, evidences this:

> CATHY (Age 17): She didn't like me going out partying…and she tried—convincing me not to go—…she would say 'please be home by two.' And I would never be home by two…it's not like you're gonna be home by two, you know, it's like—*two*? I leave at *twelve*, how am I gonna be back by two—you know?

With restrictive command statements not being enough, Cathy's mother resorts to pleading with her daughter not to go out. When it becomes apparent that these appeals will not be heeded, Cathy's mother attempts to set curfew limits by pleading for her to be back by 2:00 a.m. Cathy denies both the legitimacy and feasibility of her mother's pleas and ignores the restrictions on leaving as well as the 2:00 a.m. curfew. In so doing, Cathy has promoted herself in the family hierarchy by refusing to keep a child's place in that she refuses to comply with her mother's restrictions over her time away from home.

When the breakdown of parental authority reaches a point where resorts to pleading are to no avail, family members may then resort to the use of physical coercion. When a parent uses physical coercion in attempting to restrict the daughter from leaving the house, the daughter may counter with physical force:

> MONICA (Age 17): I remember one night, they [friends] came to pick me up and—I was—running down the stairs to go out the house—my aunt was blocking one door, my dad was blocking the other, and my grandma was blocking one—I said okay, you know, who do I go for—so, I went—I went to try to go through the door my grandma was at—and it ended up—I didn't hit her, but it ended up, I pushed her—out of the way—to go out there, because they're [friends] honking, I'm like 'shit, I wanna get high, oh my god,'—next thing I know, my dad has me by my hair on the floor, 'you fucking little bitch—don't you *ever* hit my mother,' you know—so it was really bad—so I ended up not going out that night.

Monica's parents are apparently unable to gain compliance with prohibitions on going out, and thus resort to physical coercion by blocking the doors. Monica attempts to counter with physical force, but the parent's physical force prevails. Because of physical strength, using physical force to challenge girls' attempts to go out generally only works when the challenger is a male.

When there is a breakdown in authority, physical force may prevent overt attempts of a girl to go out, but it does not address covert attempts. To counter covert attempts to go out, parents may resort to more manipulative measures in attempting to restrict their daughters from going out, such as maintaining locked doors and keeping close reign on the keys. However, the girls may counter with various strategies, as illustrated in the following scenario in which Mara's grandmother keeps all of the doors locked and carries the keys with her on a chain around her waist. Mara finds a way to remove the keys without being detected:

> MARA (Age 16): I would sneak out the house...she [grandmother] watches movies on the floor on the mat, and she falls asleep...she likes holding me when she sleeps—like I'm her teddy bear...when she fell asleep...I acted like I had fallen asleep...I pushed the hook, and I pulled it off...I held the keys with me...I wiggled away from her...and she just turned back over. I had the keys and I ran to the back door, and I unlocked the door, and I came running back and I um I slipped them on her and...I'll just act like I'll turn on my t.v. in my room...and I'll go to the back door, and I'll just leave for like two or three hours and she won't even know I'm gone, she'll be asleep, and I'll come back—and I'll—get the keys again and lock the door, and she'll *still* be asleep.

The fact that the grandmother has resorted to such extreme measures indicates that she is aware that her authority is not intact and must resort to more coercive measures. When informal control mechanisms break down in an institution, more formal measures of control will be assumed—further exacerbating and complicating relationships. The grandmother's practice of keeping all of the doors locked and the keys around her waist symbolizes the breakdown in parental authority. A simple prohibitive command and honoring of that command is apparently not enough to gain the granddaughter's compliance to prohibitions on going out. However, whereas an institution is equipped to effectively exercise such surveillance measures, the family is not set up to effectively exercise coercion. Pure coercion (with no trust and legitimacy) is generally an unreliable method of maintaining control in a family and home (Goffman 1971). Covert challenges to parental authority generally do not lead to overt friction between daughters and parents as long as the measures remain undetected by the parent.

Coming into Contact with the System: Calling Police to Help Restore Authority

One way that family conflicts over parental authority may contribute to placing girls at risk for initial contact with the juvenile justice system is when parents solicit assistance from police. Police often serve as mediators in family conflicts well before the girls actually enter the system. When attempts to try to restore authority internally by resorting to mechanisms such as pleading, bargaining, and physical coercion have failed, these parents frequently appeal to the police as a means to restore or reestablish parental control. At least initially, the police reaction is primarily symbolic—they are constrained from and/or hesitant to react punitively by making arrests; rather, they 'talk to,' lecture, cajole the girls into behaving. The following scenario provides an example of how this unfolds. Mara's grandmother began calling the police to her home when Mara was 11:

CARLA: What did she used to call the cops for?

MARA (Age 15): When we wouldn't listen to her.

CARLA: And she—what would she say when she called them?

MARA: My—my grandchildren aren't listening to me—they don't wanna do what I tell them—I don't want them here.

CARLA: And they would come out to the house?

MARA: And they would pull us outside and just talk to us and that was it... Umm—maybe about twelve times...The *same* ones would come...They said, 'we're always coming over here, your grandma's always telling us something new, or it's always the *same* thing. And you know what?—It's always something stupid, and we're tired of you guys not listening to your grandmother—they're old—your grandparents are old—they—they—they should be retired, they should be—just kicking back in rocking chairs, and you guys shouldn't be— they shouldn't be handling you, and we think we should take you away— and—' I'd be like, 'No—no—no—no—I'm gonna be good, I'm a listen to my grandmother, don't take me away, I don't wanna go anywhere.—'

The police responded by lecturing and threatening Mara and her brother with 'we think we should take you away.' Just as a breakdown in family solidarity may result in parents' mechanisms for asserting authority becoming more progressive, the same may be true for police techniques attempting to restore authority. When lecturing and threatening seem not to be effective, police may resort to scare tactics in attempting to restore parental authority:

> MARA (Age 15): They [police] were forever like, 'you ain't got no fucking respect for your grandmother, and you're gonna end up in the Halls, and you don't know what it's like—people—be um—people be *raping* people, and-'...they were just like constantly in my face...cussing at me—they were *basically* trying to scare me...but it never worked.

Similarly, Cathy estimates that before she entered the system, her mother called the cops to the house approximately twenty times. While the specific points of contention ranged from not washing the dishes to staying away from home for extended periods of time, her mother's overall complaint was that Cathy did not listen to her and did not follow her rules:

> CATHY (Age 17): She's called them before, but for stupid stuff like I didn't wash the dishes...I got home late...I didn't come home...total times, she's called the cops I'd say around...maybe twenty...just for incidents like I didn't come home, and—stuff like that or—you're not listening to your mom—you're not following the rules—stuff like that...They would just tell me 'well, listen to your mom, just begin-'—just like whatever—and they just wanted to leave—they were like 'well ma'am...we have things to handle—we have things to do—you just can't be calling us for *this*.'

These excerpts illustrate how the police, at least initially, treat these calls as interpersonal problems rather than as criminal matters. However, just as these families turn to more coercive measures when their authority fails, so do the police. When less coercive tactics fail, police may consider arresting and processing the matter as a criminal case, bringing the girl officially into the juvenile justice system. The following is an example of what happens when the police run out of patience in these situations. In this example, Mara's family calls the cops for a third time to report her as a runaway. While the first couple of times, the cops simply retrieved her and returned her home, the third time they threaten to take her to juvenile hall:

MARA (Age 15): So I was just sitting in the cop car, and I was *crying*—I was like 'no I don't wanna go to the—um—Juvenile Hall—I don't wanna go, I don't wanna go,' they were like, 'well that's it—that's your last chance, this is your third time running away, and—um, we're sick of being called, and we're tired of all this bullshit and da-da-da-da-da,'...my aunt comes over, and it's—you know—my aunt's sitting there *crying* to the cops, '*please* don't take her, she'll be good, she'll be good, she'll be good.'...'just let her come home with me, and she'll be—you know—she'll start acting right... she [aunt] convinced him, and then...They let me go under the condition that I stayed at my aunt's house, and I said 'okay.'

This time when the family called to report Mara's running away, rather than doing the usual and returning her home, the police prepare (or at least feign preparation) to take her to the police station for processing. Mara's aunt's intervention once the police arrive on the scene illustrates how family may influence whether a girl enters the system in the first place by influencing police decisions about taking her in for processing. In this instance, although the aunt was the one who initially called the police, she diverted her niece from entering the system at this time by meeting the cops on the scene and persuading them to let her niece go home with her. This also illustrates the amount of discretion that police have in determining when to cease treating a family conflict as a personal matter and to instead begin treating it as a criminal matter.

Struggles Culminating in Assault Charges: Relabeling Domestic Disputes

Previous sections of this chapter explored the types of family conflicts over parental authority and how a breakdown in family solidarity/internal order of family may lead to parents soliciting help from outside authorities. This is often many of the girls' initial contact with the system before they actually enter it, and this section will explore how these family conflicts over authority may result in the girls actually entering the system. Although some have found that with respect to runaways, the police's net of social control does not appear to be widening, others suggest that police discretionary powers allow them to circumvent the restraints of deinstitutionalization in other circumstances (Acoca 1999; Acoca and Dedel 1998; Austin and Krisberg 1981; Chesney-Lind and Shelden 1998, 2004; Klein 1979; Lemert 1981; Mahoney and Fenster 1982; Mayer 1994). This happens when the police relabel family conflicts/domestic disputes as assaults. This section explores the processes by which relabeling of family conflicts into assaults occurs.

Family-related assault charges often represent the highest degree of escalation in family control struggles. By the time assault charges occur, struggles over parental authority have been ongoing for some time and have reached a breaking point. By the time families reach this point, their attempts to establish authority through conventional mechanisms (routine commands and/or requests) or through less conventional methods (pleading, bargaining, or manipulation) have failed. Parents then resort to attempting to exert parental authority with coercive physical control, which is likely to be countered with similar physical resistance from the daughters. Earlier examples in this chapter described instances where parents called police to their homes to restore order, and police responded by going to the homes and talking, cajoling, or threatening the girls. In situations where the girls may use physical force to counter parental attempts of controlling with physical force, both parents and police seek a restoration of order by removing and detaining the girl at least temporarily. Many girls either enter the system with assault charges or are subsequently incarcerated for these charges after having already entered the system.

While there may be evidence of assault in some cases, in many cases, there often seems to be a lack of evidence supporting these assault charges and these instances often seem to be opportunities for parents to appeal to the juvenile justice system for assistance in their overall control struggles with their daughters. When police arrive on the scene, they are much more likely to believe the parent/guardian rather than the girl's version of what transpired. Countering coercive physical control with physical resistance presents the opportunity for parents to begin the process of having disobedience classified as 'delinquent.' By changing the plea from 'she won't obey me,' to 'she assaulted me,' this gives police something upon which to act. Many of these family assault charges seem to have one theme in common. They seem to involve a parent, usually the mother or woman guardian, attempting to physically block the daughter from taking some kind of action and the daughter's subsequent push to resist the parent's restraining action. This sometimes results in the parent alleging assault.

As the following narratives illustrate, it is not uncommon for family assault charges to emerge from the most contentious point underlying control struggles—a daughter's freedom to leave the house or 'go out.' For example, in the following narrative, Renee describes what happened when she returned home to pick up some items after one of her extended periods away from home:

> RENEE (Age 16): So we went back to my house, and I was picking up my makeup…shampoo…lotion…And—my mom's like, 'no, this isn't a motel, you're not just gonna come in and out whenever you please, you're only *fourteen*,'…she was really upset…she was trying to keep me in the house… and—basically I—I pushed her. I had a whole bunch of stuff in my hands, like all these bottles and stuff—and I pushed her out of my way when I was coming out of the bathroom…then…they [parents] called the police…'… she needs to stay here,'…'she's out of control,' and he [stepfather] would not let me go anywhere…the police came, and I was cussing them out… they arrested me…they're like 'well, I'm getting you for battery on your mom,'—'battery on my mom, I didn't do anything to her'—'You pushed her, didn't you?' I'm like 'yeah.' Shit—okay, they got me for battery.

In this situation, the parents attempted to restore authority in the family by calling in outside authorities (police) to remove and detain Renee. Being able to come and go as one pleases is distinctly an adult prerogative. Renee's mother suggests her frustration lies in part by Renee not keeping a child's place in the family order when she says 'you're not just gonna come in and out whenever you please, you're only *fourteen*.' In this case, it is not just that Renee is not keeping her place by coming or going as she pleases, she has returned home with concrete justification for parental attempts to police her sexual activities—a boyfriend. In attempting to prevent Renee from leaving the house again, her mother first attempts to block her and Renee responds by pushing her out of the way. Her stepfather then intervenes to block/restrain Renee while they call the police and continues to block Renee from leaving until the police arrive. This illustrates the power of police influence in defining a situation upon arriving on the scene, and in defining what constitutes a criminal act—in this case, battery. This also challenges previous conclusions that the consequence of deinstitutionalization was a narrowing and restricting of police discretion and social control.

Similarly, the following excerpt illustrates how conflict over leaving the house/going out also resulted in assault charges. In this instance, Teresa does not adhere to her mother's restrictions on going out; consequently, Teresa's mother resorted to attempts to manipulate the situation by making it more difficult for Teresa to leave the house. Since getting dressed is a precondition of leaving the house, by placing Teresa's clothes in her (mother's) closet, Teresa's mother attempted to keep Teresa from leaving. This made it more difficult for Teresa to leave the house because Teresa would have to go through her mother to retrieve her clothes. The following illustrates what happened when Teresa attempted to retrieve some items of clothing before she left on one of her extended stays away from home:

> TERESA (Age 16): So, she took my clothes—she put it in…the closet in her room—so that I couldn't get to it. And I needed something to wear that day, so I went to—the closet—in *her* room—and I was going to get my clothes—so she walked to—over from her bed—and she tried to block me—she tried to hold the closet door closed. And then…she tripped over my little brother's toy that was on the floor…that's when she called the police…she said that I hit her, and almost made her fall.

Teresa's mother's attempts to gain authority over Teresa's leaving the house by manipulating placement of her clothes failed and resulted in Teresa's mother resorting to coercive physical control. However, in attempting to block Teresa from retrieving her clothes from the closet, either her mother tripped or perhaps some sort of altercation occurred prompting her mother to trip. Either way, the event provided the opportunity for Teresa's mother to gain assistance in her overall authority struggles with Teresa by constructing Teresa's actions as being serious enough to warrant removal from the home and detention. The police had come to the house twice before in response to Teresa's mother's call and, as with this time, indicated that they found no evidence to apprehend the daughter. It seems that the mother's persistence and suggestions that her daughter was out of control may have influenced the police to take her in for processing and incarceration in Juvenile Hall. In this case, not only was there no evidence of assault when the police appeared on the scene for the third time, but the charges were subsequently dropped because Teresa's mother did not show up in court to testify.

While family control struggles seem to most commonly occur between parents (primarily mothers) and daughters, these struggles may also occur between the girls and older siblings:

> BRENDA (Age 15): I had got into it—the one—the brother (age 23) I said I don't like—one day—um—my mama had found some Weed in my room—and I had got mad and then—I started cussing and stuff—and he don't like me cussing—especially with my mom right there—so like I cussed, and I ran outside—and [he] came behind me—and he was like holdin' me—he threw me on the ground, and he started holdin me—like—and I started kickin him and stuff, and he was still holdin me…I was just kickin him so hard, and he slipped…he slapped me… he didn't mean to do it—I was just kickin him so hard, and he slipped… then I went to go get a knife, and then I called the police—then they end up takin' *me*…he always big and bad like when I ain't got noth- ing—but if I like pick up a stick then he wanna move back—so I picked up a knife…and then the police came…I threw the knife before they came and my sister—let me know –she like—'the police out there,'…I just threw 'em (knife) down—and then they came and—and they— took me.

One of the interesting dimensions of this scenario is that when the police arrived on the scene, the struggle had subsided and there was no knife in sight:

> CARLA: They didn't even *see* you with the knife.
> BRENDA: They sho didn't—that's what—like the police—he came to court too—he said he didn't see me and um—my attorney [public defender]

was telling 'em—he was like 'if she wasn't swingin' the knife—it can't be assault with a deadly weapon.

That the police were ready to remove Brenda with no apparent evidence of struggle raises the question of the basis for removing Brenda from her home:

> BRENDA: My mom told 'em like—she need a break...she told 'em that um—like 'take her cause she goin' crazy,'...At trial, my mom was telling him [judge] like—she just wanted me gone for like two weeks just to—give me a lesson or whatever—and she was just sayin' stuff like—she wanted me home...she just wanted to give me a lesson—but my judge—he was like—he ain't goin for none of that—he deal with all my mama' kids—like most of 'em—they done been in here...he was like—'what makes you think if I release you—like you ain't gon' be like them and get in trouble again?' So, he was like 'nah—I'ma keep you.'

Continuing the pattern revealed in previous narratives, this particular control struggle provided an opportunity for Brenda's mother to appeal to authorities for 'a break' in her pleas for them to remove Brenda. Age/minor status of the girls leaves them powerless in defining what actually occurs when the police arrive on the scene. The tradition of upholding parental authority over the rights of children results in authorities nearly always accepting the parent's or guardian's definition of the situation. While filing assault charges may be one strategy that a parent or guardian uses as a last resort to gain help in their overall control struggles with their daughter, in most instances they only intend for their daughters to be gone for short periods of time, such as a short-term stay in Juvenile Hall to 'teach her a lesson.' This is particularly the case for those parents who are familiar with the way the system works. However, the above passage illustrates how sometimes this strategy may backfire. In this situation, the judge sentenced Brenda to incarceration because he perceived a lack of authority in the home. This continues the juvenile court system's established traditon of intervening and assuming guardianship in families deemed lacking the appropriate authority to uphod the moral order.

Brenda's situation breaks with the general pattern of girls not being incarcerated after their first contact with the system/first arrest if the parent is willing to take them home. This illustrates how a judge's sentencing decision may be based not on the girl's offense, but on the judge's perception of whether the internal order of the family's authority relationships is intact. In this situation, the judge's decision to incarcerate Brenda seems to evolve from a sense that Brenda's family lacks a viable authority structure, based on the fact that several of Brenda's siblings had previously been in this judge's court.

How Control Struggles May Shape Differential Juvenile Justice Outcomes

Not only are many girls in the system for status offenses, but also a substantial number of girls are in the system for violating court orders. Many of these acts of violations of court orders are in essence status offenses, such as running away, and so on. Previous literature suggests judges' use of violations of court orders as a technique of 'bootstrapping' girls into detention (Costello and Worthington 1981). Once a girl enters the system, control struggles are reproduced as violations of probation, and with each of these violations, punitive measures are likely to increase. Whereas 'going out' and/or running away were not crimes before the girl entered the system, once in the system (on probation), 'going out,' especially for extended periods of time, now becomes a violation of probation, or in other words, 'going out' against parental prohibitions now becomes a crime.

Just as family control struggles may contribute to placing a girl at risk for entering the system, these struggles may also influence differential outcomes after she enters the system. Once the juvenile justice system becomes involved, it is not uncommon for the judge to consult with the parent before rendering a decision. A parent's input may influence whether a girl is able to come home or whether she is institutionalized after arrest. For example, if a parent stipulates to the judge that her daughter may come home if she abides by her rules, then the judge may send the girl home on house arrest. House arrest is a more severe measure than simply being placed on probation since it prohibits the girls from leaving the house for any purposes other than school. For this reason, house arrest would appear to be a favorable measure for parents in their struggles to control their daughter's time spent away from home, or 'going out.' However, this is rarely the case. Because many of the girls' entries into the justice system are predicated on family authority struggles, house arrest often fails because nothing is done to address the underlying control struggles:

> MIRANDA (Age 14): House arrest—that couldn't even *fade* me…House arrest cannot fade me, cause I would be at home, and I'm supposed to be in the house—I would *leave*—I'd just get up and *leave*.

Sentencing a girl to house arrest represents the court's attempt to reinforce parental authority by supplementing parental prohibitions with court-sanctioned prohibitions; thus the penalties for disobeying restrictions to go out are much harsher. House arrest adds another layer of authority, assuring more punitive consequences for the girls' strategies to gain more freedom away from home. More specifically, house arrest makes the girls' extended periods of time away from home crimes for which they can be incarcerated, which usually means recurrent stays of approximately 30 days in Juvenile Hall.

Alternatively, if a parent/guardian refuses to accept the girl back home, the judge may institutionalize her or send her to a group home:

> MARA (Age 15): They said 'Okay, then we're gonna let you go on probation,' and my grandmother ended up saying 'No, I don't want her home. She can't listen to me…she doesn't obey me, she's always answering back… I don't want nothing to do with her.'…so…they arrested me. They put me in a soda pad [temporary home] and gave me a couple more court dates. And my grandmother still said she didn't feel I was changing, and she didn't want me home. So, they put me in placement.

Mara's grandmother confirmed that at the court hearing, the judge was ready to release Mara home with probation, but the grandmother refused to accept her. Not yet willing to sentence her to incarceration or placement outside of the home, the judge placed her in a temporary shelter and she was given a couple more court dates, giving the grandmother a longer time to reconsider. Only after the grandmother seemed steadfast in her decision not to accept her granddaughter home did the judge sentence her to an open placement (group home).

While sentencing to a foster home or open placement (group home) is considered to be a viable alternative to incarceration, for many girls in the juvenile justice system, it is often the first step to eventual incarceration. Girls who are sent to foster or group homes rather than returning to their parent's home face the same dilemmas. Control struggles are often reconstructed in foster and group homes, which are deemed community alternatives to incarceration. Not surprisingly, the girls want the same freedom of action that they wanted at home, while the foster parents or group home staff wishes to establish authority and curtail girls' freedom:

> SABRINA (Age 18): Yeah—it was two of 'em—parents [foster parents]—they were like pastors at a church. And it was just like something I wasn't used to, and it was like I couldn't be myself—you know?—I'm the type of person where I like to blast my music, I like to—smoke cigarettes, I like to—go out partying, and I like to talk on the phone—and they wasn't having it, and I didn't—like it—you know? So, my social worker made an agreement with me—'well, this is gonna be your curfew—you do whatever you have to do on that when you're out,'—you know?—and it worked for a little bit, and then I got tired of it, and—I left [after about six months]…I went to a group home…I—AWOLed and I never went back…finally turned myself in to my social worker, and she took me to *another* foster home.

Sabrina's social worker attempts to ease the standoff between Sabrina and her foster parents by suggesting, if not implying, to Sabrina that in exchange for abiding by her curfew, she may do whatever she wishes during her time out/away from the home. This practice of 'don't ask, don't tell' about activities while away as long as home by curfew was also a tactic some mothers used after release, which resulted in diminishing, if not eliminating, control struggles. Because of these control struggles, Sabrina went from a foster home, to a group home, to a foster home, then back to a group home.

Just as the standoff between girls and their parents often results in the parents' reliance on the justice system, the standoff between girls and group home staff often results in staff reliance on the system when there is a breakdown in authority:

MARA: And I went to S. for my first [group home]...all girls...And so—they were trying to get us to go to a boy's [group home] and have this dance...I didn't want to go...And you know, I just said 'Well, if you take me there, I swear, I'm just going to go off on everybody there, you know, and they ain't gonna like it. So they [group home] sent me to a mental hospital. And the mental hospital—I didn't want to go there...and I ended up staying there for 2 weeks...I got sent back to [group home]. And I didn't want to go back to [group home], and they [group home] ended up keeping me again, and...when I came back, they were trying to get me to go to school. I was like 'I'm not going to school,'...they took me to [Juvenile Hall] trying to you know—admit me in, and [juvenile hall] said they couldn't take me...So they took me back to the [mental] hospital. In the hospital, I stayed there a week...the one I liked—the exact same one. And—I stayed there for a week, and—the [group home] came to pick me up again. I told them 'No—I'm not going back. I am **not** going back.' So I refused [group home], and [juvenile hall] just came, and they picked me up right away.

Group home control struggles result in girls moving from institution to institution (often from group home to group home), with incarceration in juvenile halls in between each group home. This occurs not because the girls commit new offenses, but because the same control struggles that took place between parents and daughters take place between group home staff and the girls.

Discussion and Conclusion

Through family struggles over power, these girls are largely classified as delinquent through their families' appeals to the justice system to help them restore authority. The parents (primarily mothers or woman guardians) act as informal agents of control until a breakdown in family solidarity prompts appeal to more formal measures of control. In many instances in attempting to restore their authority with their daughters, these parents form collaborative arrangements with the justice system to either threaten the girls into obeying parental authority or having the girls removed by detention if they do not act accordingly. While nearly all families have these struggles, the mechanisms and options utilized by families depend on their social locations along hierarchies of race, ethnicity, and class. The most marginalized along these hierarchies are less likely to have resources other than appealing to police and the justice system. Additionally, unlike those at other social locations, these families are in environments that more readily bring them in contact with police. In finding that family dynamics often generate what is officially considered an offense, this research supports previous literature suggesting that some 'deviance' is in large part the product of the response (thus construction) of the group, either family or community (Becker 1963; Goffman 1971; Lemert 1951; Perrucci 1974).

The system's response to these parents' pleas for help shows continuation of historical practices of state intervention into the families of children perceived to come from environments regarded as unregulated and lacking in appropriate values and structure thought necessary to foster obedience, self-discipline, and hard work. Whereas in the nineteenth century, children of immigrant families who had ethnic backgrounds different from those of established American residents were primarily the target population of excessive state intervention, in the twentieth and twenty-first centuries, these demographics have shifted to children of primarily African-American and Latino families. While intervention in the nineteenth century was primarily imposed from the outside, these contemporary parents (lacking alternative familial or community resources) are themselves calling the police, thus initiating state intervention.

While there are previous studies on how macro structural factors may converge to shape fractured emotional attachments between parents and children in impoverished African-American families (Duncan et al. 1994; Henriques and Manatu-Rupert 2001; Leadbeater and Bishop 1994; Sampson and Laub 1994), there are no studies of how these factors may shape problematic authority relationships in these families. In the larger structural context, it makes sense that the girls compete for adult status in their families since many of the circumstances they often navigate entail the complexities of adult circumstances. Simultaneous intersecting structures of race/ethnicity, class, and gender converge to place African-American women and Latinas in positions of extreme powerlessness. While the powerlessness of African-American women and Latinas has been acknowledged relative to the larger society, the powerlessness of these women in their own communities and in their families has been less explored. These women have no power and are often struggling economically and emotionally just to survive.

To the extent that challenges to parental authority play an instrumental role in the girls' coming in contact and moving through the justice system, this suggests the continuing significance of status offenses (offenses that would not be considered wrongdoing if committed by an adult) in the arrest and incarceration of girls, even though the 1974 Juvenile Justice and Delinquency Prevention Act officially deinstitutionalized status offenses. The findings in this chapter suggest that not only has the problem of differentiating youths whose actions are more affronts to parental and local authority than violations of law not been resolved, but challenges to parental authority are now being constructed and processed under other 'official' categories of crimes or delinquencies.

The family dynamics revealed in this chapter play a significant role in the girls' contact, entry, and movement through the justice system and are important not only for implications for the continuing significance of status offenses, but also for subsequent program and policy planning for girls in the system. The data in this chapter suggest the extent to which families lack resources to navigate these conflicts. Certainly, the institution provides a remedy to the most contentious element of the family control struggle 'going out,' by locking the girls in; however, the institution's resources and measures for ensuring discipline and obedience are not something that can be transferred to the family. As reflected by one mother's comments to her daughter, 'well, of course you get up and go to school here [institution], you have a whole team of people to help with that.'

Family dynamics can be placed in a larger structural context of marginalization. Economic deprivation strains relationships, often in subtle ways. Family conflicts occur within families at all locations in the hierarchical structure; however, being positioned at the bottom of the hierarchical structure poses added pressures that exacerbate any potential for conflict. In the larger structural context, economic and social factors act as stressors influencing control struggles between parent(s) and girls such that each party is not able to live up to societal expectations of the role of child or parent, thus resulting in a breakdown of authority. The girls' lives are structured such that although in age they are supposed to be kids, because of a lack of family resources, they have encountered circumstances that most adults in the general population will live a lifetime and never encounter. Ultimately this is about what it means for a child's life when the lives of their parent(s) lack the resources to provide enough of a cushion to afford their children the opportunity to live a child's life. The most beneficial community programs would not primarily target 'delinquency'; rather, they would target neighborhood economic and social conditions. Within this context, community programs could provide resources for mediating family conflict so that the families do not have to rely on the police.

Finally, we have little understanding of how socio-economic structures in general, and marginalization in particular, shape family dynamics. If power struggles are key processes through which girls make contact and enter the justice system, more ethnographic research is needed examining family conflicts.

References

Acoca, L. 1999. Investing in Girls: A 21st Century Challenge. *Juvenile Justice* 6: 3–13.

Acoca, L., and K. Dedel. 1998. *No Place to Hide: Understanding and Meeting the Needs of Girls in the California Juvenile Justice System.* San Francisco: National Council on Crime and Delinquency.

Andrews, R., and A. Cohn. 1974. Ungovernability: The Unjustifiable Jurisdiction. *Yale Law Journal* 83: 1383–1409.

Arthur D. Little, Inc. 1977. *Responses to Angry Youth: Cost and Service Impacts of the Deinstitutionalization of Status Offenders in Ten States.* Washington, DC: Arthur D. Little, Inc.

Austin, James, and Barry Krisberg. 1981. Wider, Stronger, and Different Nets: The Dialectics of Criminal Justice Reform. *Journal of Research in Crime and Delinquency* 18: 165–196.

Balck, Annie, and F. Sherman. 2015. *Gender Injustice: System-Level Juvenile Justice Reforms for Girls*. Portland, OR: The National Crittenton Foundation.

Bartollas, Clemens. 1993. Little Girls Grown Up: The Perils of Institutionalization. In *Female Criminality: The State of the Art*, ed. C. Culliver. New York: Garland Press.

Becker, Howard. 1963. *Outsiders*. New York: Free Press.

Belknap, Joanne, and Kristi Holsinger. 1998. An Overview of Delinquent Girls: How Theory and Practice Have Failed and the Need for Innovative Changes. In *Female Offenders: Critical Perspectives and Effective Interventions*, ed. Ruth T. Zaplin, 31–64. Gaithersburg, MD: Aspen Publishers.

Bishop, Donna M., and C. Frazier. 1992. Gender Bias in Juvenile Justice Processing: Implications of the JJDP Act. *Journal of Criminal Law and Criminology* 82: 1162–1186.

Bridges, George, and Sara Steen. 1998. Racial Disparities in Official Assessments of Juvenile Offenders: Attributional Stereotypes as Mediating Mechanisms. *American Sociological Review* 63(August): 554–570.

Chesney-Lind, Meda. 1989. Girls' Crime and Woman's Place: Toward a Feminist Model of Female Delinquency. *Crime and Delinquency 35: 5–29.*

Chesney-Lind, Meda, and Randall Shelden. 2014. *Girls, Delinquency, and Juvenile Justice*. Belmont, CA: Wadsworth.

Cohn, Yona. 1970. Criteria for the Probation Officer's Recommendations to the Juvenile Court. In *Becoming Delinquent*, ed. P.G. Garbedian and D. C. Gibbons. Chicago: Aldine.

Costello, Jan, and Nancy L. Worthington. 1981. Incarcerating Status Offenders: Attempts to Circumvent the Juvenile Justice and Delinquency Prevention Act. *Harvard Civil Rights-Civil Liberties Law Review* 16: 41–81.

Datesman, S., F. Scarpitti, and R.M. Stephenson. 1975. Female Delinquency: An Application of Self and Opportunity Theories. *Journal of Research in Crime and Delinquency* 66: 107–132.

Duncan, G.J., J. Brooks-Gunn, and P.K. Klabanov. 1994. Economic Deprivation and Early Childhood Development. *Childhood Development* 65: 296–318.

Empey, LaMar T. 1973. Juvenile Justice Reform: Diversion, Due Process and Deinstitutionalization. In *Prisoners in America*, ed. Lloyd E. Ohlin, 13–48. Englewood Cliffs, NJ: Prentice Hall.

Empey, LaMar T 1982. *American Delinquency*. Homewood, IL: Dorsey Press.

Federle, K.H., and M. Chesney-Lind. 1992. Special Issues in Juvenile Justice: Gender, Race, and Ethnicity. In *Juvenile Justice and Public Policy: Toward a National Agenda*, ed. I.M. Schwartz, 165–195. Indianapolis, IN: Macmillan USA Publishing.

Gaarder, E., N. Rodriguez, and M. Zatz. 2004. Criers, Liars, and Manipulators: Probation Officers' Views of Girls. *Justice Quarterly* 21(3): 547–578.

Gibbons, D., and M.J. Griswold. 1957. Sex Differences Among Juvenile Court Referrals. *Sociology and Social Research* 42: 106–110.

Goffman, Erving N. 1971. The Insanity of Place. In *Relations in Public*, ed. Erving Goffman. New York: Harper & Row.

Gordon, L. 1988. *Heroes in Their Own Lives*. New York: Viking.

Henriques, Zelma, and Norma Manatu-Rupert. 2001. Living on the Outside: Women Before, During, and After Imprisonment. *The Prison Journal* 81(1): 6–19.

Klein, Malcolm. 1979. Deinstitutionalization and Diversion of Juvenile Offenders: A Litany of Impediments. In *Crime and Justice*, ed. Norval Morris and Michael Torry, 145–201. Chicago: University of Chicago Press.

Krisberg, B., and I. Schwartz. 1983. Re-Thinking Juvenile Justice. *Crime and Delinquency* 29: 381–397.

Leadbeater, B.J., and S.J. Bishop. 1994. Predictors of Behavioral Problems in Preschool Children of Inner-City Afro-American and Puerto Rican Adolescent Mothers. *Child Development* 65: 638–648.

Leiber, Michael J., and Jayne Stairs. 1996. Race, Contexts, and the Use of Intake Diversion. *Journal of Research in Crime and Delinquency* 36: 76–78.

Lemert, Edwin M. 1951. *Social Pathology: A Systematic Approach to the Theory of Sociopathic Behavior*. New York: McGraw-Hill.

Lemert, Edwin M 1981. Diversion in Juvenile Justice: What Hath Been Wrought. *Journal of Research in Crime and Delinquency* 18: 34–46.

Mahoney, A., and C. Fenster. 1982. Female Delinquents in a Suburban Court. In *Judge, Lawyer, Victim, Thief: Woman, Gender Roles and Criminal Justice*, ed. N. Hahn and E. Stanko. Boston: Northeastern University Press.

Mayer, Judith 1994. Girls in the Maryland Juvenile Justice System: Findings of the Female Population Taskforce. Presentation to the Gender Specifics Services Training. Minneapolis, MN.

Miller, Jody. 1994. An Examination of Disposition Decision-Making for Delinquent Girls. In *The Intersection of Race, Gender and Class in Criminology*, ed. M.D. Schwartz and D. Milovanovic. New York: Garland Press.

Odem, M.E. 1995. *Delinquent Daughters: Protecting and Policing Adolescent Female Sexuality in the United States, 1885–1920*. Chapel Hill: University of North Carolina Press.

Odem, M.E., and S. Schlossman. 1991. Guardians of Virtue: The Juvenile Court and Female Delinquency in Early 20th Century Los Angeles. *Crime and Delinquency* 37: 186–203.

Perrucci, Robert. 1974. *Circle of Madness*. Englewood Cliffs, NJ: Prentice-Hall.

Platt, Anthony. 1969. *The Child Savers*. Chicago: University of Chicago Press.

Puzzanchera, Charles. 2014. Juvenile Arrests 2012 (DOJ, Office of OJJDP, 2014).

Puzzanchera, Charles and Sarah Hockenberry. 2014. Juvenile Court Statistics 2011 (NCJJ, 2014).

Sampson, R.J., and J.H. Laub. 1994. Urban Poverty and the Family Context of Delinquency: A New Look at Structure and Process in a Classic Study. *Child Development* 65: 538.

Schlossman, S., and S. Wallach. 1978. The Crime of Precocious Sexuality: Female Delinquency in the Progressive Era. *Harvard Educational Review* 48: 65–94.

Schwartz, Ira. 1989. *(In) Justice for Juveniles: Rethinking the Best Interests of the Child*. Lexington, MA: D.C. Heath and Company.

Schwartz, I., et al. 1984. The Hidden System of Juvenile Control. *Crime and Delinquency* 30: 371–385.

Shelden, R.G. 1981. Sex Discrimination in the Juvenile Justice System: Memphis, Tennessee, 1900–1917. In *Comparing Male and Female Offenders*, ed. M.Q. Warren. Newbury Park, CA: Sage.

Sickmund, M., et al. 2013a. *Easy Access to the Census of Juveniles in Residential Placement*. Washington, DC: Office of Juvenile Justice and Delinquency Statistics.

———. 2013b. *Easy Access to Juvenile Court Statistics: 1985–2013*. Washington, DC: Office of Juvenile Justice and Delinquency Statistics.

Sussman, A. 1977. Sex-Based Discrimination and the PINS Jurisdiction. In *Beyond Control: Status Offenders in the Juvenile Court*, ed. L.E. Teitelbaum and A.R. Gough. Cambridge, MA: Ballinger.

Teitelbaum, L., and A. Gough. 1977. *Beyond Control: Status Offenders in the Juvenile Court*. Cambridge, MA: Ballinger.

Wordes, M., T. Bynum, and C. Corley. 1994. Locking Up Youth: The Impact of Race on Detention Decisions. *Journal of Research in Crime and Delinquency* 31(May): 149–165.

Young, V.D. 1994. Race and Gender in the Establishment of Juvenile Institutions: The Case of the South. *Prison Journal* 732: 244–265.

Zatz, Julie. 1982. Problems and Issues in Deinstitutionalization: Historical Overview and Current Attitudes. In *Neither Angels Nor Thieves: Studies in Deinstitutionalization of Status offenders*, ed. J. F. Handler and J. Zatz. Washington, DC: National Academy Press.

4

Horizontal Surveillance and Therapeutic Governance of Institutionalized Girls

At any given time, the more powerful side will create an ideology suitable to help maintain its position and to make this position acceptable to the weaker one. In this ideology the differentness of the weaker one will be interpreted as inferiority, and it will be proven that these differences are unchangeable, basic, or God's will. It is the function of such an ideology to deny or conceal the existence of a struggle. (Horney, 1967, p. 116)

Whether the girls' contact and entry into the juvenile justice system is facilitated by family power struggles is not the concern of the institutions that incarcerate them. In the institution's logic, the girls' presence in the juvenile justice system is due to a lack of appropriate cultural values; thus this understanding serves the basis for how the institution regulates ('rehabilitates') them. Institutions serve as the locality at which the molding of citizens occurs. Previous research on how power is enacted through institutional practices provides insights about the significance of these sites in shaping citizen-subjects. Social institutions reproduce citizens and citizenship status through processes of attempting to impose dominant societal meanings/discourses (Cruikshank 1999; Garland 1997; Glenn

© The Author(s) 2017
C.P. Davis, *Girls and Juvenile Justice*,
DOI 10.1007/978-3-319-42845-1_4

2002; Foucault 1965, 1977, 1978, 1983, 1988; Rose 1988). These meanings are represented in an institution's logic, as reflected in documents, programs, policies, and daily practices.

This chapter examines the processes by which this institution reproduced a model of gendered and racialized citizenship through therapeutic discourses and techniques regulating women's sexual morality and perceived emotionality. Discourses regulating sexual morality and emotionality are part of broader discourses of meritocracy emphasizing notions of the ideal worker-citizen as rational, thus free of 'bodied' processes, such as emotions or sexuality. Under pressure to demonstrate acceptance of institutional ideals, the girls actively participated in using these dominant ideals to police each other (horizontal surveillance) in competing for status in the institution's meritocratic social order. These processes illustrate how surveillance by colleagues not in positions of power contributes to reinforcing the power of governing authority, as well as reinforcing hierarchies of gender, race/ethnicity, and class.

Institutional Power and the Reproduction of Worker-Citizens

Research on women and therapeutic governance largely draws upon Foucault and/or Acker's Theory of Gendered Organizations (1990). Foucault's theories outline how institutional power is enacted, and citizens reproduced, through processes reinforcing dominant ideologies. Acker draws upon Foucault's theories of power to elaborate on how processes that reproduce citizens through reinforcing dominant ideologies simultaneously reproduce gender hierarchies or 'gendered' citizens. She particularly focuses on the workplace. The abstract construction of the concept of a job and the ideal worker are intertwined with the larger historical construction of the abstract concept of citizen. US citizenship status has always been intricately connected to labor status in that establishing oneself as an independent laborer has always been a critical element of demonstrating eligibility for US citizenship. In theorizing about gendered processes in workplace institutions, Acker (1990) asserts that although institutions have seemingly gender-neutral policies and programs, institutional practices reveal gendered institutional logic that reproduces gender hierarchies. According to Acker, although seemingly gender-neutral, the logic by which workplace organizations operate is inherently gendered in that it reflects understandings based on differences between sexes, with greater value being accorded to those qualities associated with being male.

Embedded in the hidden assumption of the ideal worker-citizen as male is the assumption of the ideal, gender-neutral worker and the workplace as being rational and free of 'bodied' processes, such as sexuality or emotions. In the abstract construction of job, 'the abstract, bodiless worker, who occupies the abstract, gender-neutral job has no sexuality, no emotions ...' (Acker 1990, 151). Thus, in molding the ideal worker-citizen, one way that organizations reproduce gender hierarchies is through the control and suppression of sexuality or other bodied processes such as emotions since these are seen as disrupting the ideal functioning of the organization. This is achieved through organizational logic or arguments about women's sexual morality, or emotionality, or reproducing and managing institutional members through penalizing or rewarding their sexuality or emotionality management. According to Acker, one important mechanism through which institutions regulate members is through organizational logic embedded in systems of evaluation. These evaluations are infused with assumptions about gender differences and relative accorded value, and, thus, an important element of workplace reproduction of gender hierarchies.

McCorkel (2003) was one of the first to draw upon Acker to examine how therapeutic governance is gendered. McCorkel found that despite supposedly gender-neutral 'get tough' policies, gendered organizational logic based on perceptions of differences between men and women was reflected in different treatment/punishment practices between men's and women's prisons. This was manifested in the emphasis on combining therapeutic practices with punishment in women's prisons. This focus on therapy in treatment was seen as stemming from women having 'psychologically disordered' and irrational selves. Consequently, one of the purposes of therapeutic intervention in group sessions known as 'e.g.s' was to teach the women how to control their emotions in order to have a more autonomous, rational self. McCorkel also discusses the peer surveillance of these groups. In McCorkel's (2003) view, therapeutic governance is gendered both in the division of therapeutic intervention between men and women's institutions and in using group therapeutic sessions as a forum to reinforce dominant gender ideals. However, although McCorkel notes horizontal surveillance, specifically in the context of group dynamics, she does not examine the therapeutic techniques that prompt this process. She seems to suggest that it is the presence of the therapy in itself, not specific techniques, that reproduce gender hierarchies.

Like McCorkel (2003), McKim (2008), in her study of a mandated, community-based drug treatment program for women, found that the treatment program prioritized therapeutic ways of governing its clients. However, whereas McCorkel found that the institution emphasized a disembodied, autonomous, rational self and regulated the women's emotions as part of the gendering processes, McKim found that the processes in her institution were such that they encouraged women's emotional expression. McKim also found instances of peer surveillance where 'monitoring oneself was intertwined with monitoring others' (317). However, McKim's (2008) study primarily analyzes staff discourses in their meetings evaluating the women clients, rather than the discourses of the women clients themselves, especially as they police each other. She does not examine the links between therapeutic governance, horizontal surveillance, and reproduction of gender hierarchies.

Neither McCorkel (2003) nor McKim (2008) focused on how particular discourses or therapeutic techniques may have shaped horizontal surveillance, thus reinforcing gender hierarchies. However, in her study of two residential facilities for incarcerated women, Haney (2010) attempts to examine what it is about combining the therapeutic and the penal that reproduces gendered institutional logic through horizontal surveillance. She found that women's policing of each other, specifically in the context of group dynamics, was a significant element in reinforcing gendered institutional logic in the institution that combined the therapeutic with the penal. Haney reported that women in that institution "...responded to their sense of disempowerment and injustice by turning on each other and on themselves..." (179).

In attempting to pinpoint what exactly it was about combining the therapeutic with the penal that may foster horizontal surveillance, Haney points to the nature of the discourses. She distinguishes between two types of discourses, 'discourses of need' and 'discourses of desire,' and proposes that each has consequences for how an institution regulates members and the effects of that regulation. Haney proposes that strategies of governing that utilize discourses of desire attribute members' problems to having untamed desires. They attempt to instill this understanding in members by trying to get them to see that the solution to their problems lies in regulating their wants/desires. Strategies of governing that utilize discourses of need attempt to instill in their members the understanding that their problems lie in lacking certain elements that they need to become productive citizens. These discourses provide the logic for what women need to become before they can reclaim their basic rights. Haney suggests that "as a strategy of governance, discourses of desire were more individualizing than discourses of need," (27) and thus more likely to prompt policing each other.

Haney associates discourses of desire with therapeutic regimes; thus, she attributes horizontal surveillance to therapeutic regimes because she views them as utilizing discourses of desire as a governing strategy. However, she notes at one point that perhaps the lines between the two types of discourses may be blurred and perhaps there is no distinction between what constitutes a need and what constitutes a desire. I would agree that there is a lack of distinction since processes of social construction often conflate the two (needs and desires). The findings presented in this chapter expound upon Haney's attempt to uncover the specific factors of group therapeutic processes that shaped the production of gendered citizenship through horizontal surveillance. However, these findings broaden the scope in that they go beyond focusing on institutional discourses to show how the institution utilized particular techniques to enlist the girls to use dominant discourses to regulate each other.

Race and the Construction of Worker-Citizen

Acker (1990), as well as previous literature on gendered institutions (including therapeutic governance), posits gender as the primary organizing factor in institutional citizenship processes. These studies view the historical construction of the ideal worker-citizen as rational and free of 'bodied' processes such as emotions or sexuality as solely a gendered construction evolving from the historical context of industrialization and the separation of spheres (private versus public). However, the reproduction of labor and citizenship in the USA arose out of a slave-based economy. A slave-based economy provided the foundation for reproducing racialized and gendered notions of worker-citizen ideals. The economic development of the USA relied on a racially based stratified labor system comprising labor from Africa, Latin America, and Asia. 'Racialization in the labor market has been buttressed by a system of citizenship designed to reinforce control of employers and to constrain mobility of workers' (Glenn 2002, 5).

In historical processes of the construction of labor and citizenship, a language of meritocracy (rationality, self-sufficiency, bootstrap, individual responsibility) evolved as a system of beliefs justifying the underlying racial/ethnic hierarchy of the distribution of resources, status, and power. 'Notions of which groups had the intellectual capacities to do conceptual work were similar to notions of which groups had the rational, self-governing capacity required for citizenship' (Glenn 2002, 2). Thus, discourses of rationality/emotionality have underpinnings in this context. With the rise of industrialization, ideas of cultural inferiority began replacing biological explanations for Blacks' social location at the bottom of the economic, political, and social hierarchy. Whereas under slavery, economic mobility was not an option, under industrial capitalism, chances of economic mobility were extended as an illusion. US expansion westward and the need for cheap labor resulted in similar ideologies for Mexican immigrants. Thus, hierarchies of race and ethnicity are embedded in the language of meritocracy embodying worker-citizen ideals. These justifications or rationalizations are currently manifested in explanations attributing the marginalized social location of racial and ethnic groups to lacking appropriate cultural values or cultural capital. These cultural explanations are part of the overarching ideology accompanying a competitive economic system.

Discourses of sexual morality have their roots in the construction of dominant ideals of womanhood produced during slavery. The hierarchical structures of slavery in which Black women were subjects of rape and sexual entanglements with white slave-masters shaped a dual construction of dominant ideals of womanhood. Black women were not accorded the same values of femininity and chastity as White women. White women were accorded the ideal of 'chaste virgin' and sexually pure while notions of Black women and promiscuity/whore became synonymous (Collins, 2008; Hurtado, 1996). Black women have occupied the position in the popular imagination of 'promiscuous whore,' and been disrespected accordingly (Davis 1983; Hooks 1981; Hurtado 1996). This dichotomous construction remains a dominant idea that permeates the web of institutional structures. This construction of sexual (im)morality evolved to include many women of color, as well as white women at the bottom of the socio-economic hierarchy. Thus, contrary to assertions of the literature on gendered organizations, regulating sexuality and emotionality are not merely gendered phenomena.

Theoretical Frameworks

This institution's reinforcement of worker-citizen ideals through group therapeutic sessions reflects Foucault's (1977, 1978, 1983) conception of how power is constituted through the processes of disciplining thoughts. Power operates through imposing a definition of the nature of the self and circumstances that is consistent with the definitions and interests of governing authority. Foucault hypothesizes that a critical element of processes of social control and discipline is placing individuals' everyday lives under surveillance through the imposition of language that reflects and emphasizes dominant ideologies. This imposition of dominant meanings works to enact institutional power by encouraging particular self-conceptions of ideal citizens that are in line with institutional expectations, thereby instituting a form of self-policing. This process negates the need for more coercive forms of power. These dominant ideals are embedded in institutional structures; thus, power is enacted through an institution's processes, including programs, evaluations, policies, and routine practices. Foucault's (1977) 'web of discipline' proposes that discursive power operates through an institution's various actors. The findings in this chapter expand upon Foucault by providing an example of the ways and extent to which institutional subjects are *themselves* actively involved in perpetuating the process of molding subject-citizens.

These findings also expand upon Foucault's (1965) notion of modern therapeutic practices as moralizing therapy, where subjects are condemned as violators of social norms whose morals should be reformed. However, Foucault's conception of moralizing therapy does not emphasize the significance of moralizing therapy in a group-based forum. To this extent, Durkheim's emphasis on the significance of social occasions or public forums as a means of reinforcing moral codes/community beliefs provides a useful framework for analyzing dynamics in group therapy sessions of this institution. Durkheim believed that public forums of punishment served the necessary function of preserving a society's social order by clarifying a society's norms and boundaries of acceptable behavior. This process affirms collective identity and beliefs, and inhibits future deviations from these norms and boundaries of acceptable behavior. This institution uses group therapy sessions as a public forum in which to clarify and reinforce dominant meanings reflecting the greater societal moral/social order.

Goffman's (1959) framework of impression management is useful for understanding how the group therapy sessions, as forums for evaluating and demonstrating the girls' acceptance of institutional ideals, fostered horizontal surveillance. Goffman (1959) conceptualized everyday interactions as being tantamount to stage-plays in which each exchange (occasion of social interaction) entails an expression whose function is to convey a favorable impression of self through demonstrating acceptance of dominant societal ideologies. According to Goffman, the arrangement of performances will be guided by the prevailing norms of that society, which will serve as the symbols of exchange. As mentioned in chapter 1, Goffman (1959) notes the significance of a meritocratic society in shaping actions/interactions and notes how upward mobility involves the 'presentation of proper performances...through utilizing the proper symbols' (36).

In a meritocratic system or society, navigating place in the social order entails employing discourses or symbols of meritocracy to construct an ethical self. This encompasses a form of self-policing, perhaps better known as internalized oppression. Self-policing and horizontal surveillance are best captured in the literature on internalized oppression/

subordination (Fannon 1967; Freire 1970; Memmi 1967). Internalized oppression occurs when members of oppressed groups accept and incorporate images of them fostered by the dominant group in society. It involves internalizing the false belief that the system is correct or inevitable. This leads the oppressed to enforce the oppressor's guidelines—both with self and in relations with others. In a meritocratic structure in which progress and worth are always relative, self-policing is a form of competition for place in the social order. Self-policing inevitably incorporates policing others (O'Grady 2005) in the constant incentive to rank one's own behavior in the hierarchical structure. Thus, self-policing is mirrored in individuals' relationships with others through practices of using dominant ideas to police others.

Policing others constitutes a form of self-policing in that it is a way to manage a favorable impression of oneself in the hierarchical structure by signaling oneself as someone who does not possess the qualities of the target of policing. By policing others, one manages favorable impressions by appearing to adhere to institutional expectations, rules, and norms, thus indicating worthiness of favorable standing in the institution's social order. However, ultimately, it is the *impression* of acceptance of the dominant ideals that has significance, regardless of whether the citizens/prospective citizens have actually accepted the ideals. The group therapy sessions served as social occasions or public forums that provided the girls opportunities for demonstrating acceptance of institutional ideals in competing for place in the meritocratic social order. The institution used various techniques for enlisting the girls to use these discourses to monitor each other. I refer to these practices of policing others with dominant ideas as horizontal surveillance.

Models of a Gendered, Racialized Citizen

This institution reproduced a model of gendered, racialized worker-citizens through mandated group therapy sessions. As Acker (1990) notes, institutional citizenship processes are reflected in an organization's evaluation processes. Like Acker's discussion of how job evaluation processes served as a primary locale of the operation of power and reproduction of hierarchies, group therapy sessions in this institution exemplify Foucault's (1977) notion of an 'Examination.' According to Foucault, the examination was a mechanism through which hierarchical observation and normative judgment were combined, thus establishing a visibility through which subject-citizens were differentiated and judged. Foucault (1977) considered the examination to be a primary location of modern power because it combined 'the deployment of force and the establishment of truth' (184). Group therapy sessions served as this institution's primary vehicle for imposing discourses of truth.

Group therapy sessions served as forums of evaluation or 'examinations' for fitness for citizenship. The labor in this institution entailed the production of a new (moral) self through adopting institutional ideals of meritocracy entailing regulating emotionality and sexual morality in attaining institutional status of citizenship. Thus, the horizontal surveillance (utilizing dominant ideals to police and sanction each other) was a way for the girls to define themselves as being closer to the attributes of the ideal worker-citizen (worker-citizen = autonomous white male) and to distance themselves from their subordinate status as incarcerated Black and Brown girls.

The therapy sessions in this chapter mirror larger historical processes determining fitness for citizenship in that they serve as forums in which Black and Brown girls must engage in conceptual 'work' to demonstrate fitness (rationality, sexual morality, etc.) for citizenship. Notably, one of the therapists commented to me that these girls are not actually 'capable' (i.e., lack the mental capacities) of any 'real' therapy. He said he viewed the purpose of the sessions as being to foster communication. The critical distinction in thinking of evaluation processes in a meritocratic system as part of a gendered and racialized structure is recognizing that these processes are not just the result of the prejudiced beliefs of those who govern, but are embedded in the institution's logic; thus that structure is reinforced whenever the institution engages in the evaluation process (Acker, 1990).

The processes shaping gendered, racialized citizens in this institution evolved through the following interconnected mechanisms: underlying organizing structure of a hierarchical merit system; discourses of women's sexuality and emotionality, as well as discourses of individual responsibility; and group therapeutic techniques in which therapists enlisted the girls to use institutional discourses to govern and rank each other. Therapeutic techniques to enlist horizontal surveillance included the following: using each girl's initial group therapy session as a mechanism for teaching the defining of self and each girl through their offenses or past activities; using resisters as examples/targets by framing a girl's resistance in ways that suggested the resister was placing herself above others in the social order; validating hierarchical competition by joining in the chorus of girls' sanctioning as if one of the girls; encouraging the girls' snide or sarcastic comments made on the side to be introduced as part of the evaluation process of group therapy sessions; and undermining solidarity of the girls by discrediting any supporter of a resister.

One way to understand how power operates in an institution is to examine the discourses or logic through which those in charge make sense of institutional members' problems (Haney 2010). The logic or discourses that an institution employs to make sense of institutional members' problems provides the blueprint for how the institution governs, as it establishes boundaries for areas perceived to be in need of regulation. I would add to this that understanding how power operates in an institution also requires examining how institutional members make sense of and employ institutional logic. The following sections will examine the models of citizenship embedded in the institution's discourses of individual responsibility, women's sexual morality, and women's emotionality. These sections will also examine how these models of citizenship are embedded in the institution's group therapeutic practices enlisting the girls to use these ideals to police each other. In essence, these examinations reveal the varying ways that the girls utilized symbols of meritocracy to foster the impression of reproducing themselves as ethical citizens.

Moralizing Discourses: Regulating Individual Responsibility

Discourses of individual responsibility provided the groundwork for discourses regulating women's sexual morality and emotionality. The processes of shaping a subject-citizen's self entails instilling in the subject-citizen a sense of individual responsibility for developing a self that is consistent with governing interests (Foucault 1977, 1983). An important element of the institution's exercise of therapeutic power in molding gendered and racialized citizens was shaping the residents' perceptions that attaining institutional ideals was solely a matter of individual will and responsibility. Thus, in regulating the girls' sexual morality and emotionality, the institution attempted to convince the residents that their circumstances flowed from a lack of appropriate moral values and that the solution lies in their efforts to acquire those moral values. This is consistent with Foucault's (1965) description of moralizing therapy as making the madman 'feel morally responsible for everything in him that may disturb morality...' (70). Embedded in these ideals of individual responsibility are the meritocratic ideals of bootstrapping (that it was up to the residents to pull themselves up out of their current circumstances).

One technique for reinforcing ideals of individual responsibility during group therapy sessions was for the therapist to use his or her own life stories of overcoming circumstances as examples of the merit of individual responsibility:

> Mr. F. (therapist/PO) told the girls 'In order to be helped you first have to want to be helped...' He then gave himself as an example (he said he used to have a drinking problem), saying that one day he had just looked around and decided that he was better/wanted something better & decided he wanted to change...

The language of experts is not the language of objective science, but is, in essence, the language of moral authority reinforcing the moral order (Foucault 1965). Mr. F.'s language reflects discourses of personal responsibility ('In order to be helped you first have to want to be helped...') and rational decision-making and free will (he...'decided he wanted to change'...). The language of conversion (i.e., he once was lost but now is found) enhances authority of the expert. The girls then take this language that they learn through examples set by therapists and reinforce it during group therapy sessions:

> Rhonda began by asking the girls to help her. She said she was trying really hard & she needed their help. They began with a litany of comments to the effect that they could not help her if she did not try to help herself. They

seemed exasperated with her & they began to recount events (one earlier that day) in which her behavior indicated that she really was not trying... several girls in the group reiterated that no one could help her until she first helped herself...

In getting the girls to take responsibility for the circumstances by seeing the problem as completely lying within themselves, they relinquish institutional responsibility or consideration of the role of structural elements. Thus, discourses promoting ideals of free will, individual responsibility, and self-sufficiency are an integral part of institutional dominant discourses shaping subject-citizens. Previous literature (Rose 1988, Cruikshank 1999) draws upon Foucault in noting the prevalence of discourses of individual responsibility ('responsibilization'), particularly in programs of intervention for at-risk populations during the growth of neoliberalism.

Moralizing Discourses: Regulating Women's Sexual Morality

One way that the institution shaped a gendered, racialized model of citizenship regulating sexual morality was through discourses of prostitution. This was most evident in discourses indicating that prostitution was considered the most heinous crime and was the criterion that sparked the strongest responses in evaluating and regulating the girls:

> STAFF: 'You really have to watch them though. I mean some of these kids have done some really serious stuff.' I said 'really?' (thinking that he was about to speak of rape, murder, etc.) He nodded and said 'yeah, I mean we have some prostitutes in here.'

Discourses of prostitution reflect the institution's techniques of reinforcing women's sexual morality through the ranking of crimes. That prostitution is considered the most heinous offense speaks to not only the moral basis, but also the gendered and racialized nature of the institutional logic governing regulation. However, ideologies in and of themselves do not convey power. Rather, power lies in the enactment of these ideologies. Power lies in instilling in subject-citizens a definition of self that is consistent with the state's definition (Foucault 1977, 1978, 1983). The perception that prostitution was the most heinous of crimes was mirrored in the girls' self-conceptions:

> [CARLA]: ...do you feel—that in some kind of way, that what you're in here for is worse than what other people are in here for?
> RENEE: Yes. I do—I really do...after like my eyes have been opened, you now, like—I knew it was wrong...I know it wasn't like ladylike to do...I'd rather—assaulted somebody, than be on the streets and have people run up in me...people are so used to like 'oh yeah, I'm here for assault and battery or attempted murder,' whatever, or GTA, you know, and that's nothing. Because you know, it's just a—a crime. Like a—I don't know how to explain it, but it's not like the same...it's not the same as like prostitution...

The girls adapted perceptions of self that mirrored the institution's perception through the practice of adapting the institution's ranking of crimes. Renee is, in effect, saying that being a woman who violates sexual codes is a greater offense than any crime (e.g., assault and battery, attempted murder, GTA) and violates acceptable moral standards of what it means to be a woman ('ladylike'). Self-policing resulted in policing each other (horizontal surveillance) as well:

> TERESA: I don't think it's gonna help me, because—the majority of these kids—they're here for prostitution or—drugs—and I have nothing to do with that—I'm just here because _ I committed a crime out there of assault and battery...everybody else is in here for prostitution or drugs. And it's like—dang—I'm in here with just drug addicts and some prostitutes... It seems like every day, we get a prostitute...I mean I'm surrounded by prostitutes...

In the reproduction of the social order, institutional power lies in the extent to which governing authority can get the girls to form a perception of self (and others) that is consistent with that of governing authority's. Teresa reinforces the moral order through the defining/ranking of self in comparison to others ('I mean I'm surrounded by prostitutes.') In this moral order, her offense of assault and battery accord her higher status than drug addicts and prostitutes, and in her comment she draws this contrast. Objects of disciplinary control internalize norms and become monitors of their own behavior (Foucault 1977).

However, this is not solely a gendered phenomenon. It is not just the low status of women that makes prostitution so stigmatized in the social/moral order. It is also about race. In the historical construction of womanhood, there was a dual construction based on race—'white goddess/black she-devil, chaste virgin/nigger whore, the blond blue-eyed doll/the exotic "mulatto" object of sexual craving' (Rich 1979, 291). In this construction, black women and promiscuity/whore became synonymous (Hurtado, 1996). Because poor black women occupy the lowest status along hierarchies of race, class, gender, they are the most stigmatized and thus any category associated with this social location is perceived as posing the greatest threat to the moral order.

Moralizing Discourses: Regulating Girls' Emotionality

As Acker (1990) notes, the disembodied, ideal citizen is not only free of sexuality, but free of emotions as well. The institution's techniques also used discourses of emotionality to reproduce a gendered and racialized citizen. One of the ways that ideas of women's emotionality were manifested in these discourses was the constant use of the word 'drama' to refer to the girls. The perception of the innate nature of girls as being characterized by excessive displays of emotion was reflected in recurring staff characterizations of the girls as 'drama queens':

> STAFF MEMBER: She was a drama queen. She was a major drama queen...she would go to her room and she would have these little episodes...she needed attention—all the time...

These elements have a broader societal context in that the label 'drama' is often used in the broader society as a derogatory characterization reflecting images of excessive or inappropriate displays of emotion. The essence of drama (theatric, cinematic, etc.) has two defining dimensions: fictional or unreal, perhaps exaggerated depictions of reality; and containing some quotient of emotional content beyond what is acceptable in the daily navigation of 'real' life.

These dominant understandings are reflected in staff perceptions of the girls as displaying emotions beyond what is acceptable. The implication is that the girls' concerns were something they created—not real concerns of substance but fiction, somehow trivial. For example, the common concern of expressing emotions over romantic relationships was often held up by the staff as evidence of the girls' being governed by their emotions.

> The new staff person added that the girls would always be crying over some boy, while she had never seen a boy cry over a girl. She frowned & repeated, 'they just *cry* over some *boy.*' Ms. F. nodded, enthusiastically agreeing. She said that when she came there, she had thought that she would be working with boys.

The staff person expresses her disdain for the display of emotions by emphasizing the word *cry,* while simultaneously indicating girls' irrationality by suggesting girls' inability to distinguish matters significant enough to warrant such emotion ('over some *boy*'). That girls are seen as ruled by emotions and their relative position in the hierarchy is reflected by the staff person comparing, thus suggesting, that boys are in control of their emotions (she had never seen a boy cry over a girl). The policing of emotions by staff in this institution mirrors the processes regulating emotions in the workplace in the construction of accepted ways of being a model worker-citizen. The staff person's last sentiment reflects a recurring theme in staff narratives of a preference for working with boys. A preference for working with boys is one way that staff reinforced notions that girls are emotional:

> STAFF: ...In the Halls, I loved workin' with the boys—that's where I was for sixteen months and then they stuck me with the girls—when I found out—I cried. That night that they gave me my letter and told me that

you're gonna be workin' with the girls startin' such and such date—my whole attitude for the rest of the night was really sour and then—when I got ready to leave, I just cried...because I *knew* how it was gonna be...the girls *always* have problems—you always see staff runnin' over to the girls' cottages—*all the time*—or you hear about it—'them girls is off the hook— we had to *spray* somebody—'... they'll be callin' the staff...'we need your third to go over to such and such cottage...a girl is outa control,' and I'm like—'Jesus no.'...

This narrative reflects recurring themes of underlying elements comprising discourses of girls' emotionality. One gets the sense that working with girls is an environment of continuous heightened state of alert (...the girls *always* have problems ...*all the time* ... always see staff runnin' to girls' cottages). The implication is that the girls lack control ('them girls is off the hook...' '...a girl is outa control...') and thus need to be controlled. This perception of lack of control is further exemplified in her account of the need for additional forces brought in from the outside ('we need your third to go over to such and such cottage...') to subdue the girls in an attempt to regain control ('...we had to *spray* somebody'). Indeed, the impression is that conditions are so bad working with the girls that circumstances call for appeals to a higher authority ('*Jesus* no...') than mere human backup forces to subdue the girls. These accounts of working with girls evoke images tantamount to battle scenes, in which physical battles are the foundation. The expression that the girls were somehow 'out of control' suggested perhaps physical violence was at play here. However, upon further inquiry, narratives revealed that verbal expressiveness was at the heart of perceptions of the girls being out of control.

A recurring theme was that girls = drama, and this drama was somehow related to verbal expressiveness. In attempting to tease out any connections between discourses of girls' emotionality and verbal expressiveness, I asked the school principal whether he noticed any differences between girls and boys in the frequency in which they were cited for misbehaving in class. He thought about it and responded:

School principal: 'well, the girls seem to be more temperamental...' He said this slowly—thinking—as if he either wanted to qualify this or make sure that it was placed in the appropriate context, then added—'the girls seem to be more temperamental, but I don't know if that's because they're just more verbal in expressing themselves…'

In these discourses of girls' emotionality, expressing oneself verbally gets categorized with notions of excessive display of emotions. The underlying theme evolves into a sentiment of—'are they emotional or is it just that they talk a lot—emotional—talks a lot—it all runs together…what's the difference?' These sentiments echo those of authority in the rest of the institution with respect to attributing an underlying propelling force of girls' institutional navigation to their emotionality ('temperamental'). In essence, the dominant perception was that the innate inability of girls to control their emotions manifested itself through excessive (uncontrollable) verbal expressiveness. Regulating emotions through regulating verbal expressiveness is embedded in intersecting hierarchies of gender, as well as race/ethnicity. In her study of Black women navigating academia, Fordham (1993) explored the significance of talk in navigating status in institutions. Fordham found that in navigating the academy, successful Black girls achieved academic status through intentional silence. Fordham explains that this is because in order to be successful, they must pass at being the ideal student-citizen, that is, White male, embodied by the utmost sign of rationality—lack of emotions. Expounding upon Fordham, verbal expression inevitably carries the potential for revealing emotions. This is particularly the case for those at the bottom of hierarchies of race/ethnicity for whom navigating daily life requires suppressing accumulated layers of pain emanating from their devalued status. Verbal expression increases the possibility that this pain will surface in the form of emotions. These processes result in successful members of a stigmatized racial/ethnic group being simultaneously silent and *silenced* by the institutions they navigate. Of course, it is not the case that White men are necessarily void of emotions; however, it is the case that their display of emotions is far less likely to call into question their capacity for reasoning and rational judgment.

While verbal expressiveness was a target for regulation in all of the girls, African-American girls were particularly targeted on this front.

This was manifested in the staff and girls' using 'loudness' as a criteria for exclusion and policing African-American girls:

> Ms. B. asked who wanted to work and Diedre (African-American) said that she did. Diedre said she had a question for Teresa (African-American)... Diedre said that she was trying to be Teresa's friend, and she asked Teresa why she didn't talk to her anymore. Teresa responded by telling Diedre that she (Teresa) didn't know what Diedre was about yet and that she wanted to wait and see what Diedre was about first. Teresa said 'you know you came in here talking about you changed your ways, and I'm just waitin' to see whether you really changed your ways or not...and from what I've seen, you still loud...So I'm just waitin' to see whether or not you changed your ways—what you all about first...'...Diedre said that she was tired of people saying she was loud. Diedre said that she was sorry if she didn't come from a nice neighborhood like the other girls. She said she was from the ghetto and people were loud in the ghetto...'"You not staff—if the staff think I shouldn't be doing something, then let them tell me—if the staff think I'm too loud, then let the staff tell me—you not staff.'

Just as drama is a symbol of excessive display of emotions, loud also symbolizes excessive display of emotion through modulated voice tones. Thus, attempts to regulate voice may be seen, in part, as attempts to regulate emotion. Teresa is evaluating Diedre regarding whether she (Diedre) has demonstrated that she has accepted and is working to modify this perceived deficiency. 'Loud' embodies dominant ideas (stereotypes) about those at the bottom of the hierarchical structure: loud is equated with ghetto; 'ghetto' is a term used to describe those associated (or actions associated) with being at intersections of the bottom of race and class hierarchies. Diedre's reminding the girls that they are not staff reflects the extent to which power operates horizontally in that the girls assume the surveillance of governing authority. Staff does not have to assume sole responsibility for discipline because the girls reinforce dominant ideals in policing each other.

Placed in a broader societal context of how these dominant discourses function as criteria for policing, the following exchange illustrates how 'loud' is intertwined with dominant meanings of race, within this institution as well as in the broader society:

...one of the staff entered with an African-American girl who was to be a new girl in the cottage...Roxanna (Latina) who was sitting to my left said 'Oh *man—another* Black girl. We have too many Black girls.'...Jackie (African-American) and Brenda (African-American) began talking about how every time there were Blacks around, Mexicans would always think that they (Blacks) were going to be loud...Jackie said 'In the Halls, the staff be like "No talking" and they be looking at all the Black girls and the Mexican girls be steady talking and they don't say anything to them. But they always be looking at the Black girls because they think the Black girls gon' be loud.' Sonya said 'They always think—whenever they see Black people—they always think they gonna be loud.' Brenda (African-American) said 'I *know* I'm loud—and I ain't gon' change.'... Brenda (African-American) and Jackie (African-American) continued talking about how whenever Blacks came around people would either be afraid of them or think they were loud.

The girls share their experiences in the broader society to legitimize their use of dominant racialized ideals to draw exclusionary boundaries, policing each other. The conversation was a complex combination of jest and complaint about being feared...being too prominent...always being watched. These processes of policing each other mirror historical, as well as current, processes in the broader society that rationalize the location of racial minorities at the bottom of the socio-economic hierarchy by attributing this status to cultural deficiencies. 'Loud' is advanced as an inherent (seemingly natural), culturally deficient trait of being Black (compounded by simultaneous intersecting structures of class and gender). The intersection of race and gender is reflected in that just as the institution and girls sanction each other for violating ideals of womanhood with respect to chastity, the same sanctioning occurs with respect to dominant ideals dictating that respectable women should be seen and not heard. Thus through utilizing these dominant discourses of emotionality, the girls simultaneously reinforce hierarchies of race, class, and gender even though these are stereotypes associated with their own social positions in the broader society. In her study of Puerto Rican gang girls, Campbell (1987) revealed how girls used denigrated aspects of their identities to insult each other. However, Campbell focused on these insults as a mechanism for identity construction, rather than as a mechanism for negotiating power. The criteria used for policing are about much more than constructions of identity. Through these interactions, the girls are negotiating power and status in an institution that both reflects and reinforces competition for resources/status in the broader society. The girls' dominant discourses of loudness mirror the previous narratives of staff's dominant discourses associating the girls with excessive verbal expressiveness and being out of control.

Regulation of emotions is reflected and reinforced through the institution's formal practices of evaluating the girls' attitudes, as reflected in a daily form filled out by staff, with each girl's name and a place where the staff person for each shift ranks the behavior of that girls for the shift: options are 'fair,' 'good,' and so on. For example, one day, on a form that was completed by the morning shift person who left at 2:00 p.m., it said something to the effect of 'so & so ran a fair program this morning' and then gave a three-line description of the minor's behavior. I noticed that next to one name, Ms. T. had written 'minor displayed negative attitude when leaving the shower.' It is noteworthy that her sanctions are not for any overt wrongdoing or misbehavior but instead based on the minor's attitude in navigating her morning routine. In the daily evaluation of the girls' merits, failure to demonstrate the appropriate attitude results in failure to accumulate merit points. These interactions also reflect previous literature's assertions regarding how displays of deference may be more significant than actual wrongdoings in determining sanctions by social control agents (Becker 1963; Rollins 1985).

Just as dominant perceptions of girls being 'naturally' inclined to instigate conflict due to their innate emotionality was manifested in the staff's narratives making sense of the conflict, these ideologies were similarly manifested in the girls' narratives:

> ANDREA: …It's gonna be drama…it's just like—we're all girls—so, we're gonna take our anger out on each other.

Similar to expressions in previous staff narratives, in Andrea's understanding, the conflict evolves from girls' inherent emotionality and the consequent expression in sanctioning other girls. In using these dominant meanings to sanction and draw hierarchies, girls reinforce these ideas, thus reinforcing the system of existing power imbalances.

Just as staff perceptions of girls' emotionality lead to their privileging working with boys over girls, so do girls' perceptions of girls' unreliable emotions and untrustworthiness lead to the girls privileging the company of boys, thus further distancing themselves from the devalued status of being a girl:

> Monica & another girl said that [on the outside] they would rather hang around kicking it with the guys, rather than girls. Monica said if she saw a lot full of girls & then a lot full of boys, she would pick the guys any day. A lot of the other girls, particularly Miranda agreed. Monica continued by saying that when you talk to girls about things, they just go on forever. A few of the girls laughed & nodded their heads. Monica continued by saying that when you say something to a girl, she takes it to heart & holds a grudge—she emphasized *forever*. Monica said she didn't hold a grudge. If you told her something she would be over it & that was that. She said 'but girls just take things to heart & hold a grudge forever.'

The message is that girls are untrustworthy as comrades because of their emotionality (holding a grudge) and she simultaneously defines and distances herself from the devalued status of the category (i.e., by contrast, she does not hold a grudge). The implication is that boys are able to control their emotions and thus do not hold grudges, and she is more like a boy in that she is able to control her emotions. Once again, the emotional realm of not being able to control their emotions incorporates verbal expressiveness perceived as uncontrollable talking ('when you talk to girls about things, they just go on forever').

This disparaging of emotions can be illustrated with the way that Miranda views love. Miranda views love as a loss of control and portrays love as being ruled by emotions. This is exemplified in the following exchange in which she elaborates upon the perceptions of women's weakness evolving from emotionality by suggesting how women's inferiority as a result of emotionality is manifested in their relations with men:

> MIRANDA: They are *so* stupid…they hoish—they can't control their little emotions…fall in love with every nigga they go with…then there's the females who like—who let niggas—I aint even gon' lie—that's what really annoys me about Sabrina—how she let her nigga whoop her ass after she tried to commit suicide over that nigga…girls wanna be all cuddled up and everything…

The use of dominant ideologies to demean other girls is a symbolic way to 'move up' hierarchically to the position of boys. In talking about other girls' perceived weaknesses, the girls are punishing themselves while simultaneously moving away from their stigmatized status. If they can criticize it, it is assumed they are not it. As reflected in the previous staff narrative in which girls were demeaned for crying over boys, Miranda similarly demeans girls for displaying emotions over men. Miranda expresses an annoyance with the perceived weakness of what it means to be a woman: not to be in control of one's emotions—to be under the control of men, as exemplified by 'falling in love.' This perceived lack of control is further emphasized by suggesting an indiscriminate pattern of girls' object of affection: it is not just that they fall in love, they fall in love with *every* man, suggesting that they do not possess the rational faculties to choose. Further, Miranda's comments suggest that she even views the abuse as the by-product of Sabrina's lack of control of emotions/falling in love.

Techniques Reinforcing a Gendered, Racialized Model Through Horizontal Surveillance

While the institution's organizational logic provided a foundation for power, institutional power is enacted or negotiated daily through micro-level interactions and practices. One technique that the institution used to enlist horizontal surveillance in the reproduction of institutional ideals was using each girl's initial group therapy session as a mechanism for teaching the significance of judging each other through the ranking of offenses. This technique entailed the practice of requiring, upon arrival, each girl's initial group therapy session as involving revealing her name, age, and formal charge, as well as learning and memorizing all of the other girls' names, ages, and formal charges. Through these introductions in group sessions, the institution lays the groundwork by enlisting the girls in a form of 'setting up'/identifying the problem (flawed, immoral selves), before beginning the 'work' of individual transformation making one worthy of citizenship:

> In order to get their Level Ones, two of the new girls had to go around the group and state all of their cottage sisters' names, ages, and charges. The first one to go was Cathy. When she got to Renee, instead of saying 'Prostitution,' she said 'two forty seven.' Renee turned to her and said, '*Thank you.*' During the second girl's turn, when she got to Renee, she said 'two fifty seven' and kept going. Ms. Y. said, 'Wait a minute—two *forty* seven.' The girl said 'two forty seven.' Ms. Y. said, 'Do you know what that is?' The girl nodded and said 'prostitution' and kept going.

Institutions shape citizens' understanding of themselves by imposing particular definitions of the nature of self (Foucault 1988). The institution must first establish the girls as having a morally devalued status, one unworthy of 'citizenship.' As Garfinkel (1956) noted in summarizing characteristics of successful denunciations or ceremonies of degradation, both perpetrator(s) and circumstances defining perpetrator(s) must be defined/redefined as a uniformity or 'type' that is not the norm or 'out of the ordinary' (422). Learning to identify themselves and their colleagues by their official charges is one of the first lessons in thinking of their circumstances in individualistic terms. This technique reinforces the notion that their charges are as important as their names and ages in defining them, thus reinforcing the message that the problem primarily lies within them. Through these initial sessions, the girls learned that using background information for the purposes of judging was a normal part of the processes of working to obtain the institution's citizenship. The fact that stating their own as well as other community members' misdemeanor charges is a requirement for attaining level one of the institution's merit system conveys the message to the girls that hierarchical ranking is a fundamental element of social mobility.

While each girl's initial therapy session provided the mechanism for enlisting horizontal surveillance through teaching to judge self and others according to offenses, subsequent sessions provided mechanisms for reinforcement. This was generally accomplished through the staff using one or more girl's resistance to institutional definitions as an opportunity to incite hierarchical competition (girls' judging). Resistance reflects the perception of irrationality of particular rhetoric (Fox 1999). In essence, these exchanges became a competition of defining oneself—defining one's worthiness for citizenship—in the social order in accordance with ideals of women's sexual morality and using each other as targets of comparison in this process of defining. One technique of using resistance to enlist competition was for the therapists to frame a girl's resistance in a manner that suggested she was placing herself above the other girls in the social order. This is exemplified in the following exchange in which the therapist frames Cathy's resistance in a manner that suggests Cathy sees herself as not belonging there—of higher status than the other girls. This prompts Cathy's and Renee's use of ideals of sexual morality to distinguish their own, as well as each other's place in the social order:

> Cathy said she was having a hard time adjusting to being here. Ms. Y. (therapist/p.o.) said, 'Could you be more specific?'…Cathy said '…this is just really affecting me.' Ms. Y. said, '*how* is it affecting you?' Cathy was crying. She said 'I feel like I'm in a mental hospital—I just can't take it.' Ms. Y. said 'Cathy, could you say how it's affecting you without insulting your cottage sisters?' Cathy continued '…And I talk to my mom about it. And she tells me to just stay to myself and not to have anything to do with the other girls.'…Ms. Y. told Cathy that while she was there, she had to learn to get along with her peers and in order to do that she had to not put everything off on her peers, but had to recognize the part she played in it. Ms. Y. said, 'Because you're presenting it as if you really don't belong here and everyone else is a criminal or a mental case. And that's insulting to your cottage sisters. You did something to get here. And you need to look at your role and what you can do to ease your stay here.'…Renee loudly told Cathy '…you're in denial Cathy and you better just start smellin' the funk—cause you're no better than the rest of us—some of the things you told me you did and the people you were hanging around with—about doing drugs and having sex—' Cathy said 'I never said I had sex.' Renee said 'Oh right—you're a virgin.' Cathy said that she hadn't said she was a virgin, but it's not like she was a prostitute.

The power of group-based forums in the molding of citizens is illustrated by the fact that whereas in Cathy's initial group therapy session (illustrated above), she avoided stating Renee's charge, by this later date, Cathy has learned and accepted the practice of using Renee's prostitution charge to compete for place in the social order. Renee uses ideals of women's sexual morality in an attempt to establish Cathy's immorality, thereby suggesting that Cathy *does* belong there. Renee does so by revealing and using Cathy's background activities as evidence. The significance of sexual morality is reflected in that Renee includes 'having sex' as one of the pieces of evidence. The implication is that having sex ranks on par with doing drugs or engaging in illegal activities. The significance of women's sexual morality is further reflected in that of all the activities Renee cited, it was the charge of 'having sex' to which Cathy responded. Renee further attempts to define Cathy's sexual (im)morality ('oh right—you're a virgin.'). Cathy counters Renee's definition of her (and thus her place in the social order), by using Renee's formal charge of prostitution as evidence defining Renee's ranking at the bottom of the social order. The implication is that while having sex may be immoral, the unofficial activity of 'having sex' at least accords her higher status than having an official charge of prostitution. It is noteworthy that Cathy does not address the charge of doing drugs; rather, it is the charge of having sex that assumes significance. Both Renee's and Cathy's comments reflect how, for girls, having sex is on par with and perhaps worse than official categories of illegal activity.

The primary practice of group sessions consisted of therapists in some way initiating the judging, then retreating to let the dynamics unfold. However, sometimes therapists utilized intervention techniques even after policing by the girls had begun. One such technique was to join the girls in the chorus of judging. Techniques involving joining the girls in the judging process once the competition was under way were likely to happen when a girl directly or indirectly challenged the institution's view of prostitution, particularly when it was perceived that the other girls' reinforcements of institutioal logic was ineffective. This was particularly salient when a girl suggested that prostitution was a viable avenue for achieving meritocratic ideals equated with citizenship:

Mr. F. (therapist/p.o) came in for group. Sabrina said she wanted to work. She said she was nervous about going before her judge and worried about to whom her judge would release her…Mara said 'you're eighteen—why don't you just live on your own—get a job'…Sabrina said 'but I'm scared, what if my money gets low?' Mara said, 'It's called a Job.' Sabrina said 'but—what is minimum wage—three something—?'…Sabrina began talking about how she didn't want to get a 9–5 job and work her way up. She began talking about how she had been on the top. She said 'I was on the *top*—…' Jackie said, 'that was just an illusion.' Dr. A. (clinical director) had already begun to lean forward on his knees to say (loudly whisper) 'Sweetheart, no you weren't—and there's a flip side to that feeling that you were on top—because you know that on the other side of that little voice in your head telling you that you were on the top was a little voice saying "you ain't nothing but a ho"'—(Sabrina had a surprised/startled look on her face & she said 'Dr. A. stop'). She sat back in her chair. Dr. A. continued by saying that she knew that was true, that that was the flip side of the voice telling her that she was on top. When he finished, Sabrina said 'Dr. A. how did you know that?' Ms. S. said, 'because he's Dr. A.' Everyone, including Dr. A., laughed…Ms. S. said, 'you needed to hear that.' Then added 'and coming from a man—you especially needed to hear it from a man—you needed to get a man's point of view.' Jackie added '*especially* coming from a *man.*' The session ended shortly thereafter.

Sabrina's resistance to institutional ideals is reflected in her assertion that she does not want to work her way up in a minimum wage job when she had already achieved a high degree of social mobility working as a prostitute. In questioning whether she could support herself on a minimum wage job, she challenges the meritocratic notion that minimum wage jobs can be a viable avenue for social mobility while simultaneously suggesting that prostitution can be a viable avenue. This prompts the direct intervention of the therapist. Both the message ('you ain't nothing but a ho') and the manner of delivery (dramatic effect of leaning toward her) reflect how value commitments are often reinforced through manipulation of emotion, consistent with Garfinkel's (1956) conceptions of public ceremonies of degradation. In essence, these group therapy sessions operate as shaming sessions. Dr. A.'s whispered voice represents the voice of authority, which is, in essence, the voice of society reflecting back to

Sabrina how society views and judges her. In her study of therapeutic group sessions of teen mothers Fujimoto (2001) also notes the significance of emotions in the therapeutic process and calls for further research on 'how institutional representatives employ emotions in the construction of "compliant" and "resistant" types of clients.' (20).

Because the sessions were preoccupied with reinforcing morality, Sabrina's practical concerns of how to raise a child on minimum wage were not addressed. Sabrina's fears (...said she was nervous ...' I'm scared'...) about navigating structural complexities (...'what if my money gets low?'...) are ignored in favor of institutional rhetoric of self-sufficiency and bootstrapping. In effect, Dr. A.'s focus on Sabrina's individual responsibility decontextualizes her circumstances. His message conveys that material circumstances are not the important issue; rather, what is important is that she uphold standards of morality. The implication in Dr. A.'s message is that somehow adapting the appropriate values will address the material concerns.

Dr. A. is reinforcing values reflecting prostitution as a grave (moral) crime, serving as a lesson reminding the girls of appropriate codes of sexuality and appropriate standards of womanhood. However, because race and sexuality have a particular social–historical context in which they are intricately intertwined, Dr. A.'s whispered sentiments carry a more nuanced meaning. As discussed previously, hierarchical structures of slavery in which Black women were the victims of rape and objects of non-emotional sexual entanglements with white slave-masters shaped dichotomous conceptions of 'woman.' The material location of working alongside men, as well as the sexual entanglement with white slave-masters, was critical in shaping a dual construction of dominant ideals of womanhood such that Black women were not accorded the same values of femininity and chastity as white women. As previously mentioned, White women have historically been accorded the ideal of 'chaste virgin,' while Black women have occupied the position in the popular imagination of 'promiscuous whore' (Davis 1983; Hooks 1981; Hurtado 1996). This historical context illuminates the significance of race and gender hierarchies in shaping the power embedded in the delivery of the message 'you ain't nothing but a ho' from a White man in a position of authority to a powerless African-American girl.

Just as therapists reinforced sexual morals, therapists used techniques to regulate and reinforce ideals of women's emotionality. Governing authority created and reinforced narratives of girls' emotionality, and girls, in turn, reinforced these dominant ideologies by utilizing them to sanction each other. One way that therapists regulated and reinforced ideals of women's emotionality was by encouraging horizontal surveillance through group therapeutic techniques that introduced the girls' judgments of each other as a basis for work in the session. This included encouraging the girls' snide or sarcastic comments made on the side to be introduced as part of the assessment or evaluation process of group therapy sessions. The following exchange illustrates how governing authority, through the processes of group therapy, reinforced girls' policing each other's emotionality:

> Renee wanted to know from Dr. A. why he had called for Roxanna to say her sidebar (mumbled/whispered something under her breath to the person sitting next to her) comment 'drama' to the whole group...Dr. A. said...he thought this particular comment was useful...Renee wanted to know how that was useful & said that if someone made a comment that was negative, it should not be asked to be repeated to the group...Roxanna said that she did not mean it to be negative. Renee...told her that it was mean...Dr. A. said that maybe she [Renee] should pay attention to the comment 'Drama' because it applies to her & that she does tend to be on the dramatic side...

Renee is referring to events of the previous evening's (mandated) family therapy session in which one of the girls whispered the comment 'drama' under her breath, not to the group, but as an aside, to which Dr. A. responded by asking her to repeat her 'sidebar' comment aloud to the group. 'Drama' serves to discredit Renee's perceived excessive display of emotions, thereby instructing Renee, as well as the group, on the acceptable expression (or lack thereof) of emotions. Renee challenges the therapist by asking the reason for his encouragement of Roxanna's comments of 'Drama.' Dr. A. responds by simply validating the assessment of 'drama' as 'useful.' Renee persists by wanting to know the logic behind his action and counters his perception of 'useful' with her own definition, 'negative.' Dr. A. counters her resistance and reinforces his definition by simply stating that the term 'drama' 'applies.' These exchanges illustrate how these sessions are primarily negotiations of competing definitions of the girls' circumstances. Through these expressions, both the woman staff person and the girls validate Dr. A.'s, and thus the instition's, definition of the circumstances. This illustrates how those at the bottom of the hierarchical structure internalize and actively participate in reinforcing dominant ideologies and hence the underlying power structure.

In these negotiations, the power imbalance prohibits recognition of interpretations other than those embedded in institutional ideals. The power of the institution in these negotiations is reflected by the fact that although Renee initially challenges Dr. A., in the end his definition of the circumstances (Renee's emotionality) prevails:

> Renee became even more upset & told Dr. A. that she hated him & said 'You always try to make me look stupid.'...Renee rattled off a list of other unsettling events & ended by saying 'and I'm on my period now in case you didn't know.'

Power is demonstrated as an entity's ability to influence interpretations of self and circumstances. In the end, the institution's definition of Renee prevails, and she publicly concedes and defines herself accordingly. In claiming, 'I'm on my period,' Renee publicly discredits her interpretations/judgment/rationality/self, attributing her logical inquiry to biological circumstances beyond her control, thus substantiating the institution's claims. Resistance is subsumed into dominant discourses such that what is taken as self-knowledge is, in actuality, knowledge of the self and circumstances that are the institution's definition (Fox 1999). 'Discourses of Truth' (Foucault 1977) prevail: if governing authority says she is emotional, then it must be true. In her frustration, her emotions surface, thus validating the institution's perception. Thus, the allegations of emotionality become a self-fulfilling prophecy.

Another technique enlisting judgement of each other was therapists showing the girls how to introduce and use each other's daily activities to evaluate each other's progress or claims of change. The girls learned through examples from therapists to use evidence from daily activities to refute or contradict claims of change, and thus to refute claims of assuming individual responsibility:

> ...Maria said...I want to stop taking my psych meds [anti-depressants] because I want to try to start doing it on my own...I told the nurse...Ms. Y. (therapist/p.o.) said 'Maria—didn't you just yesterday turn in something to staff because you were thinking about cutting yourself?' Maria looked at Ms. Y. and was silent. She said to Ms. Y. 'You didn't have to just blast me out in front of everyone like that.' Ms. Y. said that was what the group was for- to talk about issues and Maria responded that she didn't necessarily want the group to know everything because her cottage sisters, when they found out things, would just throw it in your face. Ms. Y. said 'Well, no one should be throwing anything back in anybody's face. Is that understood?...Explain to me why you told the nurse that you didn't think you needed to take your psyche meds and just yesterday you gave one of the staff something that you had to keep you from cutting on yourself?'...

In this exchange, the therapist (Ms. Y) and Maria are negotiating dominant ideals of rationality, individual responsibility, autonomy, and self-sufficiency. Evidence of Maria's daily activities is called upon to invalidate/question her ability to engage in autonomous, rational decision-making. On the one hand, by expressing her desire to stop taking her medication and '...start doing it on my own...,' Maria is proclaiming her move toward self-control and autonomy. Through her actions expressing a desire to attempt to navigate her life without medication, she conveys the impression of self-control, self-reliance, and institutional ideals embedded in worker-citizen ideals. Yet on the other hand, Ms. Y. challenges Maria's self-evaluation and decision-making by introducing information from daily activities to discredit Maria's suggestion that she is moving toward self-control and autonomy. In essence, Ms. Y is providing an example to the girls of how to use daily activities to point out contradictions between each other's words and deeds in evaluating and policing each other's (moral) progression in the social order, thus worthiness for citizenship.

Models of a Gendered and Racialized Citizen: Other Discourses of Women's Subordinate Status

While ideals of women's sexual morality and emotionality were the most prevalent discourses, discourses also included other intersecting notions of women's subordinate innate nature. For example, intertwined with notions of girls' emotionality and accompanying verbal expressiveness are notions of girls as untrustworthy. However, discourses of girls' trustworthiness are part of broader discourses of rationality reflected in notions of sound judgment. The following narrative suggests the connections between notions of emotionality, verbal expressiveness, and trustworthiness:

> SABRINA: ...on the outside, I don't hang around females...I only have one female friend that I hang with...and—we hang around with nothing but guys... females keep a lot of—drama going. Females can't keep they mouth closed. Females love to talk, females love to brag, females just—can't be trusted. Now, if I tell a guy something—you know what I'm saying—he can keep that to himself...I get along better 'wid' a guy, because—for the simple fact—I can tell him anything—you know—he don't look down—look at me—he don't throw it in my face—he don't do nothing—nothing like—if he's my friend—but a female—shhh—oohh, no...

Once again, girls' emotionality is perceived as intertwined with their verbal expressiveness. Like others in the institution, Sabrina attributes these complex social relations to the innate nature of girls. The message is that unlike boys, girls are not able to control their emotions, and thus are not able to control information they possess ('...females can't keep they mouth closed...' '...if I tell a guy something, he can keep that to himself'). The dominant stereotype of girls as 'two-faced' reinforced the perception of them as untrustworthy as associates. Because of the perception of the nature of girls as being unreliable holders of information, the girls were cautious in divulging personal information since it could put them at risk. Men's perceived superiority in having control of their emotions translates not only into dominant perceptions of men being more reliable in not divulging information, but also into perceptions that they are more reliable in withholding judgments ('...he don't look down—look at me...'), nor will a guy use information as a weapon (...he don't throw it in my face—he's my friend...). In essence, the perception is that men are trustworthy because they have control over their emotions, thus they can rationally think about/process information without jumping to conclusions and judging. All women are oppressed by structures that embed these dominant ideals. However, the dual construction of womanhood established notions of moral superiority of white women; thus, these ideals are most harshly used to judge and regulate girls and women of color.

The prevailing notion of girls being unreliable holders of information translated into dominant ideologies of girls' innate nature as gossipers. The perception that the natural essence of girls is as judgmental gossipers was one of the most prevalent notions of what comprised the drama. This provided yet another basis for distancing themselves from the category of 'girl' and privileging their relationship with boys:

> MAGGIE: ...on the outs, I have one road-dog and a whole bunch of boys that I kick it with...sometimes I'll kick it with girls—like—you know—maybe smoke with 'em or kick it with 'em like that. But not *all* the time—they're just like—get high buddies *once* in a while...because they're stupid...they just do little stupid—like annoying stuff—and they talk shit...I can't be with them—and they—um—gossip—too much drama...

The extent of the devalued status of girls is suggested by Maggie's elaboration on the types of activities in which girls are worthy as associates ('... get high buddies *once* in a while...). The implication is that girls are mainly good for trivial, mindless activities that demand little—and even for those only *once* in a while. She sets up this assertion of women's inability to control emotions by placing it within the dichotomous construction of rationality/emotions by first alluding to girls' lack of intelligence ('...they're stupid'). This then translates into an unintelligent existence manifested in trivial actions ('...they just do little stupid...annoying stuff'), including trivial conversation ('...they talk shit...gossip...'). The implication is that girls do not say anything of substance. Once again, there is the perception of emotionality and verbal expressiveness being intertwined.

Institutional discourses also frequently included notions of women as being manipulative or 'sneaky.' Therapists reinforced these notions through techniques encouraging the girls to introduce judgments of each other based on these ideals. For example, the exchange below illustrates how a therapist reinforced these notions through engaing horizontal surveillance to solicit information about daily activities as evidence in evaluating a girl's claims of progress:

> Jackie said that she wanted to work, so Ms. A. indicated for her to go next. Jackie said that she didn't know what to work on. Ms. A. asked her how she was getting along with her cottage sisters & reminded her that previously there had been complaints from her cottage sisters about her being manipulative and pretending not to know things—so in terms of that, how was she getting along with her cottage sisters? Jackie said ok & Ms. A. asked the girls whether this was the case. The girls indicated no, it wasn't the case and one by one proceeded to register their complaints against Jackie. Maria began by saying 'I don't like her.' Ms. A. said 'why don't you like her?'… Maria looked at Jackie with disdain and said 'She (referring to Jackie) talks like a therapist.'…The group laughed…Renee and Roxanna told of a couple of other incidents which they said reflected a pattern with Jackie: Jackie would purposely do something to irritate a girl, the girl would say something to her/call her a bitch, then Jackie would go tell the staff 'She called me a bitch for no reason.' Renee and Mary were laughing. One of the girls complained about Jackie reaching over her & her food at the dinner table to get something…

Actively soliciting the girls' verification of a girl's claim for change served to encourage introduction of daily activities. This also shows the significance of informal channels of information in the formal evaluation process. By turning to the other girls for verification of Jackie's claims, the therapist is validating the girls' judging each other as part of the therapeutic ('working') process. One by one, the girls began to offer evidence in the form of daily activities to challenge Jackie's assertions of not being manipulative. In this technique, rather than offering the daily activities as objective evidence that can be used in determining a girl's progress, the girls are encouraged to go one step beyond and offer a character assessment as a framework for discussion. Consequently, this assessment becomes the point of contention or claim against which the girl must defend herself. In other words, it is as if she is guilty until proven innocent. In this process, evidence of daily activities was offered not only to refute a girl's claims of change but to help a girl come to know herself through the institution's/therapist's definition. It is the ability to introduce as evidence activities that would otherwise be privileged information that reinforces the institution's power (Fujimoto 2001). In these sessions, privileged or private setting information is wielded as a weapon to invalidate rational, as well as moral, competency, thus rendering the girls powerless to construct alternative definitions of their selves and circumstances.

The above exchanges also illustrate the trial-like nature of these group sessions in that the girls act as witnesses, introducing testimony in the form of each other's daily activities as a form of evidence in evaluating transformations of selves. By offering evidence, each girl, in effect, serves as witness for the prosecution. The trial-like nature is also illustrated by how, if there are no present charges made by the girls, prior charges can be introduced by the therapist/judge. The therapist's asking the girls to verify Jackie's assertion of improvement illustrates the power embedded in the ability of the girls to define the perception of each other and the possibility of those in power utilizing these judgments as criteria of assessment in formal evaluation processes. The arbitrary nature of these processes is reflected by the randomness of the evidence offered ('I don't like her...she talks like a therapist'...reaching over someone's food at the dinner table...). This illustrates processes of constructing deficiencies or deviances out of ordinary, everyday actions, as well as the subjective nature of evaluation processes. Just as significantly, it illustrates that it is not so much about what one has accomplished (or not accomplished) as it is about whether one is exhibiting the proper attitude of having adapted institutional ideals. In other words, it is not the content that is important—it is the attitude surrounding the content that is important. This is particularly the case in evaluation processes when there is no tangible product other than the production of self.

Staff judgments of the girls also served as a basis for enlisting the girls to evaluate each other's progress by introducing each other's daily activities. Once again, the therapeutic technique was to call for feedback from the girls in the form of offering daily activities as evidence of a girl's character assessment. The therapist's encouragement of peer surveillance in reinforcing institutional ideals is illustrated by her calling for evidence ('feedback') from the group to substantiate claims of Cathy's 'being sneaky/provoking.'

> Ms. V. asked Cathy what about the staff's comments that she was sneaky about things—was she going to say she had no idea what they were talking about? Cathy indicated that she did not know what they meant by her being sneaky, and Ms. V. asked the girls if they could give feedback to Cathy so that Cathy could understand what she was doing. One of the girls said something about Cathy saying things under her breath about other girls and when the girls said something to her, Cathy would run to staff, telling on the other girls when Cathy was the one who quietly/secretly provoked the other girl. Brenda said 'like today—under your breath, you called Teresa a bald-headed B.'...Cathy said something to the effect that she had done that and then began explaining why she had called Teresa a bald-headed B, because Teresa had said something to her first. Cathy said 'you know—I should just start saying things out loud—to them when they start provoking me and not keeping it to myself...' Brenda said 'you *should*.' Brenda then began saying something to which Ms. V. responded dismissively 'and you're the *main* one not to take responsibility.'

In this technique, it is the judgment that is offered, then the daily activities. As in the previous exchange, under the therapist's encouragement, the girls—as witnesses—begin to offer testimony in the form of everyday activities as evidence against a girl not conforming to institutional ideals. However, this time, the therapist moves to dismiss one of the witnesses' testimony by questioning *her* adherence to institutional ideals ('and you're the main one not to take responsibility'), suggesting to Brenda that she lacks the credibility to judge. Thus, ironically, ultimately because of their status, none of them is deemed to be a credible witness. This illustrates the impact of the girls' low status on their attempts to elevate their status. Since they all occupy a similarly low status, the only way they can elevate their status is through discrediting each other, and this serves to maintain and strengthen the power of governing authority. Ultimately, even the resisters end up reinforcing governing/institutional power by engaging in surveillance as part of a survival mechanism. The therapist's encouragement of peer surveillance and introduction of daily activities as evidence of progress (or lack thereof) contributed to normalizing colleague surveillance as a fundamental element of attaining citizenship.

Therapeutic Techniques Subverting Citizen Solidarity

An institution's power to reinforce dominant ideals depends upon group solidarity around those shared beliefs, and if communal members begin forming their own beliefs, this dissent poses a threat to group solidarity (Durkheim 1947[1912], 1950[1938]). In essence, institutions reproduce citizens through squelching critiques of the institution. In order to reinforce ideals and hierarchies of women's sexual morality and emotionality, therapists used techniques to get the girls to police each other with these ideals, thereby undermining solidarity between the girls. Thus, therapeutic techniques enlisting the girls to police each other included techniques to undermine solidarity between the girls. Rarely did solidarity between the girls occur, and the few times it surfaced, therapists quickly moved to disarm it. In these instances, the technique was for the therapist to introduce evidence of daily activities to invalidate the credibility of the supporter(s) of the resister, thus reminding them of their place at the bottom of the social order. This is illustrated in the following exchanges in which two of the girls, Diedre and Joyce, agree with another girl who resists partaking in the self-disclosure that is a necessary element of group therapy:

> Diedre and Joyce began agreeing with her. They said that's why they don't do it. Diedre said she told them she wasn't going to discuss her problems like that & that if she had problems, she took care of them on her own.

Diedre repeated/emphasized this & Dr. A. looked at her & moving his head for emphasis said 'Oh *yeah* Diedre, you take care of it on your own—that's why you're at level 0—that's why you're on STOP—right? Because you take care of it on your own—right?—You've got it all together and you take care of it on your own.'

Diedre and Joyce's support of Maria's resistance to disclosure poses a threat to the group's (institution's) affirmation of disclosure as a critical element in assessing worthiness for citizenship. The gravity of having not one, but three dissenters among the group is revealed by Dr. A.'s swift response to one of the two additional dissenting members. Dr. A. counters the challenge to institutional authority by introducing discrediting information about the status of one of the supporters (Diedre) of the resister, thereby suggesting Diedre's lack of legitimacy. In essence, any critique of the institution provokes from the institution the suggestion that by virtue of the criticizer's status, that person's critique is inferior, and thus invalid.

Informing on Each Other as a Form of Horizontal Surveillance

As part of negotiating status and power, the girls challenged each other's place in the system in competing for status. One way that they did this was by revealing personal information about each other—to governing authorities, as well as to each other. As Rollins (1985) points out, revealing information about others is power. Policing each other in the form of telling on each other is a way of attempting to assert authority over someone else's place in the hierarchical structure. The girls are competing with each other to show evidence of the production of new selves. Each has a stake in showing that the other girls are not producing new elements. Given that the girls have no tangible product to show in the production of selves, one way that they compete is by highlighting evidence that others are not producing the required elements of self. The following exchange illustrates how the girls draw boundaries and reinforce hierarchies through surveillance in the form of revealing information about each other to staff:

> Before group started, Ms. S. had the girls gather in a circle around the desk, and she proceeded to tell them that she was tired of them getting into each other's business by constantly telling the staff about something another girls was doing, for which the teller thought she deserved hours or didn't deserve her level or didn't deserve to be leadership. She said she was tired of it—all the telling on each other. She mimicked the girls in a whiny voice by saying, '*so and so did this—so and so didn't do her special—so and so should get hours…so and so isn't showing leadership…*'

That informing on each other was a mechanism for competing for place is evidenced by the informant's suggesting sanctions in terms of the institution's merit system (*'so and so should get hours'*). In essence, if one is unable to accrue points, at the very least, one can compete by suggesting that others do not deserve the points they have accrued. Thus, informing on each other was another mechanism for competing for place in the social order. In essence, the practice of telling on each other may be viewed as a tactic for self-promotion.

Revealing discrediting information to governing authority is a way for the girls to distinguish themselves in the hierarchical structure and to potentially impact the relative placement of other girls in the hierarchical structure. However, even when information is not revealed to governing authority but instead confined to revealing to peers, it still serves as a mechanism for power in the competition for status.

> Cathy: …she[unit supervisor] told me 'some of the girls told me you've used Ecstasy and Cocaine,' and—I—I was—you know—so I had to—I couldn't lie anymore—it's like my stuff was *everywhere* already. From telling—you know—maybe I told two girls and then they all passed it on to each other…I wasn't cautious enough—and my stuff just floated—I guess I just was depressed—I needed somebody to talk to. And I just let it out—and it was a *big mistake*. But I learned.

In her study of the policing practices of adolescent girls, Brown (2003) notes, 'Reporting to everyone and anyone…allowed the opportunity to announce her own compliance with what is considered "normal"' (142). Policing each other results in the girls being the primary enforcers or social control agents to the extent that those in power do not have to be as vehement about enforcement because the girls do the enforcing for those with power. These processes inhibit solidarity among the girls, thus inhibiting the group as a source of support in navigating the hierarchical structure or in navigating challenges:

> Maria then began to talk about how she felt ashamed about her drug problem. She said she didn't even like to talk about it in group because she had talked about it before, and one of the girls had told someone outside of the unit because at school one day, she had gotten into it with a girl from another unit and the girl said to Maria, 'At least I'm not a drug addict,' and Maria said she had felt really bad.

The use of this private information as a resource for competition is reflected in the girl's comment 'at least I'm not a drug addict'—a comparison of herself and her status to that of Maria's. This surveillance is shaped by competition for status; however, an important structure exacerbating surveillance in this institution is the merging of public and private spheres of activity. The merging of public/private spheres is a structural feature that intensifies competition by providing increased opportunities for surveillance, as well as increased opportunities for private sphere information to be used in institutional evaluation processes. This institution's ability to maintain control rests on the merging of public/private, which provides the structure for the absence of privacy. Every minute detail of the girls' lives is subject to evaluation for how it meets the criteria for mobility in the institution. Consequently, private sphere actions become the basis for merit. This institution's convergence of public and private spheres provides an inherent contradiction since successful competition in the broader society relies on the two spheres being separate. In the broader society, the historical separation of spheres, at least in theory, enabled one sphere (private) to act as a kind of refuge from the competitiveness and demoralizing aspects of the public sphere. The institution's merging of public and private spheres is a continuation of historical practices of state intervention in the private realms of those at the bottom of social/economic hierarchies.

Discussion and Conclusion

This institution created a gendered and racialized citizen through discourses regulating sexual morality and emotionality during group therapy sessions. These models of citizenship were reflected in discourses of prostitution, as well as discourses of 'drama.' Discourses of sexuality and emotionality were part of the broader worker-citizen discourses of meritocracy and individual responsibility. Group therapy sessions served as vehicles for therapists to utilize techniques enlisting the girls to use these ideals to rank and judge self and others. Although not in positions of authority, the girls actively participated in bringing resisters into line with institutional ideals. As in Acker's conception of a job evaluation, in the rehabilitation processes of this institution, group therapy sessions may be seen as an evaluation mechanism tantamount to job evaluations. In essence, each group therapy session served as a forum for evaluating the girls' progress in accepting the institution's dominant discourses and thus for assessing their ranking in the social order. The findings of this chapter reflect Foucault's (1965, 1977, 1983, 1988) conception of how institutional power is enacted through the imposition of dominant ideologies.

These forums provided the therapists opportunities to clarify ideals as well as opportunities to enlist the girls to reinforce these ideals with each other. Girls who in some way seemed to resist the dominant ideals were used by therapists to clarify and reinforce the ideals through enlisting the girls to use this example as a reference to rank self and others. To this extent, these group sessions functioned as public forums of punishment, similar to what Durkheim viewed as necessary for preserving a society's social order. Durkheim viewed these forums as necessary for clarifying a society's norms and boundaries of acceptable behavior, affirming collective identity and beliefs, and inhibiting future deviations from these norms and boundaries of acceptable behavior. Marx and Foucault viewed these processes as part of reinforcement of the underlying distribution of resources and power, thus strengthening the hierarchical position of those in power.

Previous studies have primarily focused on reinforcement efforts by governing authority. Yet although not in positions of authority, the girls in this study actively participated in bringing resisters into line with institutional ideals. More research is needed to illuminate the ways that dominant meanings are enacted, not only by governing authorities, but by institutional colleagues not in positions of authority. These findings also expand upon previous literature on institutional gendering processes by linking the micro dynamics to broader societal historical citizenship processes to suggest how seemingly gendered processes are simultaneously reproductions of race/ethnic hierarchies.

Research examining court practices reveals a history of preoccupation with girls' sexuality. This institution's reproduction of gendered and racialized citizenship through therapeutic techniques regulating girls' sexual morality is a continuation of that historical process. Controlling girls' sexual morality through punishment has its historical context in the development of the juvenile justice system's attempt to separate supposedly 'wayward' children from 'criminal' children. For girls, waywardness included perceived sexual promiscuity and the remedy was instilling values of sexual morality. The activities of White middle class women moral reformers revolved around using ideals of female sexual propriety to monitor the moral and sexual behaviors of the working class, particularly immigrant girls (Chesney-Lind & Shelden 2014). Girls who did not conform to these ideals were deemed to be wayward and in need of control through state institutions such as reformatories or training schools.

This institution reinforced colleague surveillance by setting up a highly competitive structure in which the girls demonstrated their institutional competency for citizenship by publicly reinforcing institutional ideals in the monitoring of colleagues. Horizontal surveillance is a way for those under surveillance to gain a sense of control/power—a way to affirm their worth in a meritocratic structure in which worth is relative. Through reinforcing the institution's rules, the girls demonstrate to governing authority their own acceptance of these rules, thereby providing the opportunity to make a favorable impression and elevate their own status in the hierarchical structure. These dynamics suggest how a peer governance system that encourages the demonstration of the attainment of institutional ideals through the public evaluation of colleagues fosters disciplinary mechanisms of surveillance. This also lessens the appearance of coerciveness from those in positions of authority. As a result, participants in the process become performers in order to demonstrate their acceptance of institutional ideals.

The exchanges in these sessions illustrate the particular coerciveness of evaluation processes within structures in which public and private spheres are within close proximity of each other, or in which there is no separation between public and private. It is likely that processes of horizontal surveillance are particularly heightened in circumstances where public/private spheres are merged since private sphere actions become a base for evaluation. Privileged or private setting information is wielded as weapons to invalidate rational as well as moral competency, thus rendering the girls powerless to construct alternative meanings of their selves and circumstances. The ability to introduce as evidence activities that would otherwise be privileged information reinforces the institution's power (Fujimoto 2001).

While these findings raise questions about the impact of meritocratic structures (or types) on therapeutic governance, these dynamics also raise a larger question of how merit-based rehabilitation programs may foster processes of horizontal surveillance. Further exploration is needed on the viability of 'rehabilitation' programs solely based on a merit structure in which the primary grounds for evaluation is one's attitude or acceptance of institutional ideals since these processes are more likely to premise morality as the basis of rehabilitation. In rehabilitation programs in which merit is the basis, at the very least there should be content of evaluation other than the transformation of attitude. This would be a step in moving evaluation away from morality as the primary basis of evaluation. To the extent that these findings invite the rethinking of merit-based rehabilitation programs, it moves beyond current literature on gender equity in the criminal justice system, which has primarily limited focus of the debate to comparisons between women's and men's programs.

The findings in this chapter also expand upon previous studies of therapeutic governance by studying gendering processes among adolescent girls, rather than adult women, and by studying these dynamics in a co-ed institution. This is significant because previous studies of therapeutic governance have suggested that therapeutic governance reproduces gender hierarchies through a therapeutic division of a more likely presence in women's institutions. This gendered division of therapy is explained as being a factor of gendered organizational logic attributing women's circumstances to psychologically disordered selves. The logic is that women's crimes are a factor of something wrong on the inside while men's crimes are a factor of their responses to structural/economic conditions (McCorkel 2003). However, in this institution, the therapeutic regime's gendered organizational logic of this co-ed institution is that the girls (as well as the boys) have immoral selves resulting from a lack of appropriate values, rather than 'psychologically disordered' selves. Neither the boys' nor the girls' circumstances were attributed to structural circumstances. This lack of distinction was perhaps shaped by the co-ed structure of the institution. It is possible that gender segregation shaped gendering processes in this co-ed institution such that they resembled that of single-gender institutions. Had group therapy sessions been integrated, perhaps discourses would have been more 'gender-neutral' and perhaps discourses of girls' sexuality and emotionality would not have dominated group therapy sessions—at least not to the same degree.

While on the surface these processes appear to be exclusively or primarily gendered (reproduce gender hierarchies), these institutional processes replicate broader societal historical processes that reproduce race/ethnic hierarchies. Ideals of meritocracy were historically constructed to rationalize the appropriation and social location of non-White labor in the economic development of the USA. Thus, hierarchies of race and ethnicity are embedded in the language of meritocracy (including ideals of gender) and the institution's meritocratic rehabilitation program produced a gendered as well as racialized citizen.

Placing these dynamics in the larger context of historical development of the juvenile justice system also allows an understanding of how these dynamics reflect and reproduce racial hierarchies. The juvenile justice system evolved out of the childsaving movement in which social reformers ('child savers') thought that adolescent crime stemmed from a lack of appropriate morals, more specifically, families that lacked appropriate morals. Their concerns became regulating the moral behavior of the children of underclasses, which primarily targeted/encompassed the children of immigrant families and families from different ethnic backgrounds. Immigrant families living in what were perceived as 'slum' areas in the inner cities were targets, then later the target of state intervention became the children of predominately Black and Brown families. The population in this institution exemplifies this racialized sorting/targeting in that with few exceptions, the residents of this institution are African-American and Latino. The positing of bad values as an explanation for the conditions of black families contributed to a social and political landscape in which bad black values became the primary explanation in all perceived dysfunctional behavior of Blacks.

More recently, previous literature on welfare reform has elaborated upon the connections between the reproduction of work/labor and racialized/gendered citizenship, as well as reproduction of historically constructed meanings (Frazier and Gordon, 1994). Much of this literature has noted that discourses of welfare reform reflect and reproduce worker-citizen ideals, including attributing the social location of women on welfare to a lack of appropriate moral values. Sexual immorality and lack of work ethic, including notions of control of emotions, are intertwined in these discourses. As previously noted, the effort to move women from welfare is intertwined with programs designed to instill these women with the appropriate moral values embedded in worker-citizen ideals. Similarly, this institution attempts to instill worker-citizen ideals in a population of Black and Brown girls and establishes a rehabilitation system/program in which the girls must demonstrate their acceptance of these ideals. The program of this institution was established well before welfare reform, thus the impact of welfare reform on the program is not clear. However, perhaps welfare reform heightened the emphasis on meritocratic discourses emphasizing worker-citizen ideals.

Reinforcing worker-citizen ideals as rationalizations for the girls' circumstances distracts attention from the underlying structures of state/governing power and unto the 'cultural' habits/deficiencies of the powerless. Historical and social reproduction processes (Feld 1999; Glenn 2002;

MacLeod 1995; Steinberg 1989) shaping the girls' location at the bottom of socio-economic structures make it unlikely that they will accrue significant substantive rewards of citizenship once they leave the institution. Upon leaving the institution, the girls' lives are structured such that they are overwhelmed with reacting to the daily circumstances emerging from their marginalized social locations shaped by hierarchies of race/ethnicity, class, and gender. A program that recognizes these structural conditions and helps the girls navigate these structural circumstances would be a more logical and effective approach.

Finally, these findings have broader implications for thinking about the reproduction of gender, race/ethnic, and class hierarchies on a broader societal level. They show the significance of group-based horizontal surveillance processes in the reproduction of hierarchies in merit-based systems. Further research is needed on how, and the extent to which, horizontal surveillance processes may reproduce gender, race, and class hierarchies in other institutional settings, such as workplace merit-based evaluation processes.

References

Acker, Joan. 1990. Hierarchies, Jobs, Bodies: A Theory of Gendered Organizations. *Gender & Society* 4(2): 139–158.

Becker, Howard. 1963. *Outsiders*. New York: Free Press.

Brown, Lyn M. 2003. *Girlfighting*. New York: New York University Press.

Campbell, Anne. 1987. Self Definition by Rejection: The Case of Gang Girls. *Social Problems* 34(5): 451–466.

Chesney-Lind, Meda, and Randall Shelden. 2014. *Girls, Delinquency, and Juvenile Justice*. Belmont, CA: Wadsworth.

Collins, Patricia Hill. 2008. *Black Feminist Thought: Knowledge, Consciousness, and the Politics of Empowerment*. New York: Routledge.

Cruikshank, Barbara. 1999. *The Will to Empower: Democratic Citizens and Other Subjects*. Ithaca, NY: Cornell University Press.

Davis, Angela. 1983. *Women, Race & Class*. New York: Vintage Books.

Durkheim, Emile. 1947[1912]. *Elementary Forms of Religious Life*. Glencoe, IL: Free Press.

_____. 1950[1938]. *The Rules of Sociological Method*. Glencoe, IL: Free Press.

Fannon, F. 1967. *Black Skin, White Masks.* New York: Grove Press.

Feld, Barry. 1999. *Bad Kids: Race and the Transformation of the Juvenile Court.* New York: Oxford University Press.

Fordham, Signithia. 1993. 'Those Loud Black Girls': (Black) Women, Silence, and Gender 'Passing' in the Academy. *Anthropology & Education Quarterly* 24(1): 3–32.

Foucault, Michel. 1965. *Madness and Civilization.* New York: Vintage Books.

———. 1977. *Discipline and Punish: The Birth of the Prison.* New York: Vintage Books.

———. 1978. *The History of Sexuality: An Introduction (I).* New York: Vintage Books.

———. 1983. The Subject and Power. In *Michel Foucault: Beyond Structuralism and Hermeneutics,* 2nd ed., ed. Hubert L. Dreyfus and Raul Rabinow, 208–226. Chicago: University of Chicago Press.

———. 1988. Technologies of the Self. Ed. Luther H. Martin, Huck Gutman, and Patrick H. Hutton, 16–49. Amherst: University of Massachusetts Press.

Fox, Kathryn. 1999. Changing Violent Minds: Discursive Correction and Resistance in the Cognitive Treatment of Violent Offenders in Prison. *Social Problems* 46(1): 88–103.

Fraser, Nancy, and Linda Gordon. 1994. Dependency Demystified: Inscriptions of Power in a Keyword of the Welfare State. *Social Politics* (Spring): 4–31.

Freire, Paulo. 1970. *Pedagogy of the Oppressed.* New York: Continuum.

Fujimoto, Naomi. 2001. What Was That Secret? Framing Forced Disclosures from Teen Mothers. *Symbolic Interaction* 24(1): 1–24.

Garfinkel, Harold. 1956. Conditions of Successful Degradation Ceremonies. *The American Journal of Sociology* 61: 420–424.

Garland, David. 1997. 'Governmentality' and the Problem of Crime: Foucault, Criminology, Sociology. *Theoretical Criminology* 1(2): 173–214.

Glenn, Evelyn N. 2002. *Unequal Freedom: How Race and Gender Shaped American Citizenship and Labor.* Cambridge, MA: Harvard University Press.

Goffman, Erving N. 1959. *The Presentation of Self in Everyday Life.* New York: Doubleday.

Haney, Lynne. 2010. *Offending Women: Power, Punishment, and the Regulation of Desire.* Berkeley: University of California Press.

Hooks, Bell. 1981. *Ain't I A Woman.* Boston: South End Press.

Horney, Karen. 1967. *Feminine Psychology.* New York: W. W. Norton & Company.

Hurtado, Aida. 1996. *The Color of Privilege*. Ann Arbor: University of Michigan Press.

MacLeod, Jay. 1995. *Ain't No Makin' It: Aspirations & Attainment in a Low-Income Neighborhood*. Boulder: Westview Press.

McCorkel, J.A. 2003. Embodied Surveillance and the Gendering of Punishment. *Journal of Contemporary Ethnography* 32(1): 41–76.

McKim, Allison. 2008. Getting Gut-Level: Punishment, Gender, and Therapeutic Governance. *Gender & Society* 22: 303–323.

Memmi, Alfred. 1967. *The Colonizer and the Colonized*. Boston, MA: Beacon Press.

Morris, R 1965. Attitudes Toward Delinquency by Delinquents, Non-Delinquents and Their Friends. *British Journal of Criminology* 5: 249.

O'Grady, Helen. 2005. *Woman's Relationship with Herself: Gender, Foucault and Therapy*. New York: Routledge.

Rich, Adrienne. 1979. *On Lies, Secrets, and Silence: Selected Prose, 1966–1973*. New York: W. W. Norton.

Rollins, Judith. 1987. *Between Women: Domestics and Their Employers*. Philadelphia: Temple University Press.

Rose, Nikolas. 1988. Calculable Minds and Manageable Individuals. *History of the Human Sciences* 1: 179–200.

Steinberg, Stephen. 1989, 2001. *The Ethnic Myth*. Boston: Beacon Press.

5

Family Power Struggles After Release

MARA: It's just been for the past week because I—I don't know, maybe it's just because I'm all stressed out…I took four sleeping pills the other day. I was gonna take the whole bottle but I didn't. That was last Friday. No last Thursday night I took the pills. And I didn't wanna get up. Cause Wednesday—I came home Wednesday, that day Wednesday—and J. broke up with me—my boyfriend—and I was all heartbroken and then, the police are supposedly looking for me…my grandma's constantly telling me 'the police are looking for you, the police are looking for you,' and I'm like 'no, they're *not*,' I'm like 'just leave me alone,' and then J. broke up with me and then I'm having *problems*, and—I was just *a mess*—my grandma was talking *shit* and I was like 'aw fuck it,' so I was going to take the whole bottle, but I was like, nah, I just wanna knock out for a day and get a break, you know?…Everything is just—hard for me…I feel like sometimes like giving up. Like [inaudible] the drama that I just went through—and I honestly feel like giving up.

This chapter examines the girls' family control struggles after release. The question of what happens after release is particularly interesting for this population. They are young and youths whom the court and intake staff deemed most likely to benefit from a rehabilitative treatment program.

© The Author(s) 2017
C.P. Davis, *Girls and Juvenile Justice*,
DOI 10.1007/978-3-319-42845-1_5

However, the girls are basically released with no support systems to assist them in coping with the multiple stressors of their environments and lives. Being released is highly unstructured without anyone other than their already overburdened probation officers to facilitate the process. While all of the girls want to improve their behaviors after they are released, this is a difficult task given the circumstances to which they return. The data suggest that those instances in which the girls fare best during post-release are those in which family conflicts over authority have been modified in some form. These modifications occurred when the parent, the daughter, or both made compromises with respect to parental authority.

Before illustrating how control struggles ensued after release, the following will briefly summarize the return situations of each of the following seven girls who participated in the post-release portion of the study: (1) Renee; (2) Rosa; (3) Mara; (4) Miranda; (5) Cathy; (6) Sabrina; (7) Monica. Renee and Rosa were the only girls to participate up to six months after they were released. Renee, Rosa, and Sabrina were the only girls of the seven whose family authority/control struggles were modified upon returning home, resulting in much less contentious family relations. Renee, Rosa and Monica returned to different neighborhoods since each of their families moved during the girls' latest incarceration in an attempt to sever the girls' old peer networks.

This was Renee's second time in this institution. This time, she returned to live with her mother, stepfather, and younger brother who, during her incarceration, had moved to a predominately Anglo lower middle class suburban neighborhood at least 50 miles from the neighborhood in which she lived prior to her last incarceration. This move was, in part, an effort to remove Renee from the surrounding circumstances of her previous neighborhood. Her stepfather's income afforded the family economic resources that the other families lacked (her stepfather is Anglo, thus reflecting Hurtado's [1996] argument that women who are most closely positioned to White men stand the greatest chances of access to resources). Power struggles in Renee's family were modified after she was released in that her mother allowed her to spend time away from home as long as she was home by her curfew of 9:00 p.m., which was adhered to by Renee. Adhering to this curfew was her mother's primary concern and her mother followed a policy of 'don't ask—don't tell' in terms of where Renee went during her time away as well as with whom she spent her time. Additionally, Renee was the only girl to be enrolled in an after-care program, which consisted of a three-person team whose goal was to get her off of probation. She enrolled in a continuation school almost immediately after release, attended school regularly, and was the only girl out of the seven to graduate from high school within six months after she was released.

Rosa returned to live with her mother, stepfather, sisters, and brother. While her family had also moved to a different neighborhood, it was similar to her old neighborhood in ethnic (predominately Latino) and economic (predominately working class) composition. Authority/control struggles in Rosa's family were also modified in that Rosa now adhered to her mother's strict rules that the only time that Rosa was allowed away from home was when she went to school, and after school, she had to come straight home. Rosa countered this a few times by going to spend some weekends at her father's who did not place restrictions on her time away from home. However, eventually her father told her he was going to place restrictions on her time out, so she ceased going to her father's. After a few months, Rosa's mother began allowing her more freedom to 'go out.' Rosa enrolled in a continuation school shortly after she was released and while she attended school regularly, she did not attend classes regularly and spent a lot of school time hanging out in the restroom with classmates. Although Rosa had been a heroin addict, she remained heroin free up to at least our last meeting, six months after her release.

Mara returned to the same neighborhood to live with her grandparents and while family tensions were low the first month, they subsequently resurfaced until Mara left her grandparent's home to live with her mother and her mother's boyfriend. Mara's post-release experience was conflict-ridden and her first major conflict was becoming entangled in an argument between her mother and her mother's boyfriend during a visit to their house. Mara enrolled in a regular high school—the same high school she attended before being incarcerated, but the school soon channeled her to home schooling because of the perceived risk her presence posed to the school (gang rivalries, etc.)

Miranda returned to the same neighborhood to live with her mother, father, and younger brother. Authority/control struggles with her mother resumed almost immediately over her time spent away from home (going out). Miranda enrolled in a regular high school—the same high school she attended before incarceration and enrolled in the same classes for 'emotionally disturbed' students. Miranda attended school only sporadically. She resumed smoking weed enough to maintain a 24-hour day, seven days a week high. Around three months after release, Miranda went on the run.

Cathy returned to the same neighborhood to live with her mother and younger brother. Authority/control struggles began almost immediately over her time spent away from home (going out). At three months after her release, although enrolled, she had yet to attend school. She secretly worked some evenings as a club promoter and used the money she earned as a sort of bargaining chip for her mother's silence about her activities. Cathy also resumed her use of crystal meth soon after release, although I am not certain as to the frequency and extent of use. Two days before her review court hearing, Cathy was considering going on the run because she feared that at the court hearing they would try to detain her because her P.O. might write in her report that Cathy had not been attending school and that her drug test was dirty. However, the report from Cathy's P.O. turned out to be positive, and Cathy remained free.

Sabrina returned to the same neighborhood to live with her aunt, uncle, and cousins. She was the only girl whose probation was terminated upon her release. Authority/control struggles were modified and since Sabrina was now 18, her aunt did not try to place curfews or limits on Sabrina's actions, although this did not prevent her aunt from voicing her opinions. Sabrina did not enroll in school until approximately three months after release. Soon after she was released, Sabrina met a man and subsequently spent most of her time living with him and his gang associates rather than at home with her aunt and uncle. This continued until her boyfriend was shot and killed during a drug-dealing mission. After this, she returned to spending most of her time at her aunt's, enrolled in school, and began thinking about what she was going to do with her life. Sabrina was the only girl in the study who had a child, and occasionally, on weekends, the child's father (who had custody) allowed him to stay with Sabrina.

Monica returned to a different neighborhood to live with her mother, stepfather, and younger brothers and sisters. The neighborhood was the same ethnic (mixed) composition and the same economic (working class) composition as her old neighborhood. Authority/control struggles resumed almost immediately upon release over her time spent away from home (going out). Monica enrolled in school, but only attended once or twice. Less than two months after release, Monica contacted her old peers to come pick her up, and she went on the run until she was picked up and arrested four months after her release and eventually returned to the same institution. While she was on the run, she resumed heavy use of crystal methamphetamine and she had frequent contact with her mother. She used money from her activities to help her mother pay the family's rent and to help her mother buy groceries.

Resumption of Authority Struggles

After release from institutionalization, girls in the juvenile justice system are likely to return to the same family control struggles that contributed to their entering the system or being incarcerated. These power struggles are likely to have significant consequences for the girls' quality of life after they are released, thus affecting whether they are successfully able to move off of probation. This is significant since most girls are re-incarcerated not based on new offenses, but on probation violations. Periods of incarceration are unlikely to contribute to improving family control struggles that propelled the girls into the system:

CARLA: Okay, so what kinds of things are you guys getting into about—you and your mom?
CATHY: Um—me not wanting to [inaudible] her bed, helping her clean her room, washing the dishes—cause I don't really eat at home—I eat out all the time. Because like I don't wanna—you know—I don't want her—telling me like—'oh you ate my food,'—so, I'll just go and buy my own food. You know, I really want my own place right now…honestly, I just want my own place—by myself…if she'd let me do my job—like leave me alone—I know I come home late or—sometimes the next day—but—you know, she's not giving me money…

After the girls are released, control struggles are one of the most difficult challenges with which they must contend. Many girls return to more of the same. The girls resume resenting their families' (primarily mothers') attempts to establish authority over their actions. While many of the girls return to power struggles within the family, this does not mean that control struggles remain unmodified. For example, family struggles may dissipate or be calm for the initial month, but then subsequently return to degrees of discordance similar to their pre-incarceration forms:

> CARLA: Were things different between you and your grandma?
> MARA: Yeah, everything was better.
> CARLA: It was better?
> MARA: Yeah—but in like—the last couple of weeks has just been real bad, but I know it's gonna go back to—being okay. It's because um-
> CARLA: So you two aren't arguing as much?
> MARA: No—in the past two weeks, yes, we have been arguing. But it's just—it's stupid, over stupid *little* things.

Although Mara assesses the relationship with her grandmother as being better, she qualifies this by revealing that in the last couple of weeks, there has been friction. It has been two months since Mara was released, and for the first month, there was minimal family conflict, then conflict began in the second month.

While Mara's family control struggles did not begin until the second month after she was released, sometimes the struggles form almost immediately upon release and rise to much higher degrees of tension. Unlike Mara whose family conflicts started out on a calmer note then gradually escalated, Miranda's control struggles began almost as soon as she was released:

> MIRANDA: Well—like getting in trouble by—staying out late…I go and come as I want…I'm messin' up at—not goin to school…*A lot*…I missed this whole week.

CARLA: *Oh*—so, what are you doing?

MIRANDA: *Chillin'*—and getting high and just—meeting guys and—kickin' it…I been kicked out twice, because me and my mom, we done already got into fights and stuff—like fist fights. This was on Monday. I got kicked out—and everything. But—like—you know—I came back and everything when my dad was home, because she be trippin' and she think this her house—even though she don't *pay* for shit…me and her do not get *along*—I been sleepin' and stayin' gone away from here so I could be the fuck away from *her*. Shit—she ain't *gotta* kick me out—I'm gone bitch—bye. Me and her do *not* get along. I can not *stand* her … like she made a psych appointment. That's why we got in a fight—she made a psych appointment for *me*. Knowin' dang well—I don't *get* along with psychologists.

For Miranda, post-release experiences are for the most part just as they were before she was incarcerated. She is entangled in the same family conflicts/control struggles. Tensions between her and her mother are just as strong, if not stronger than they were before. The only difference seems to be that unlike prior to incarceration, tensions between her and her father seem to have dissipated. However, parental authority still seems not to be viable, as Miranda comes and goes as she pleases. This is because it is her mother who attempts to assert authority over Miranda.

Just as before the girls were incarcerated, a great extent of their family control struggles centered on the girls' freedoms to spend time away from home. This remains a central focus of the struggle after the girls are released:

MONICA: I had just got out, so my mom was still kinda tripping, like—you know—'oh, you're already trying to go out, and—' blah-blah—whatever… So, I started getting really like—I don't know—like—just anxious—I wanted to leave the house—I started going out a lot. I don't know—I would get mad—we started arguing—and I started drinking a lot—I was drinking like every day. I mean—my mom *knew,* but she *didn't* know. Like—cause I had bought a bottle of gin—and I just had it in the house, and my mom—she wasn't tripping—it was like—for the weekend—you know—to go party with some people. But I started drinking like everyday, because I couldn't—I didn't want to do drugs, because Ms. L.

(probation officer)—would show up randomly to my house to test me…I did not wanna get violated. So, I was just drinking…So my mom wasn't tripping but—she was only mad because I wasn't going to school. That-
CARLA: [interrupting] Did you have a curfew?
MONICA: Yeah—she tried to put twelve o'clock on me, but—that never happened—we would—me and my sister would pour into the house like two or three in the morning.

In this case, Monica is not following two out of three of her formal probation rules—she is not going to school and is not abiding by any curfew and her mother seems unable to enforce Monica's adherence to either going to school or going out. Although she is drinking regularly, technically, this is not a detectable violation of her probation terms.

One of the reasons that parents wish to restrict their daughter's time spent away from home is to restrict contact with both old and new peers who may negatively influence them. The next passage illustrates how with technology, the girls do not necessarily have to leave the house to make new peers:

MONICA: I met this girl Callie on the internet—cause she said she was bi-female, and I was like—'oh, let me talk to her—let me see what's up with her,'—so…she calls me, and she's like 'I wanna meet you,'—you know—'me and my boyfriend—could we go pick you up—I wanna meet you,' and I was like 'well, I don't know,' I was like 'I just got in trouble cause I just got a tattoo,' this and that—she's like 'oh—you have a hook-up?'—cause she was the same age as me—we were both—you know—seventeen. And she's like 'oh,' you know, 'I wanna get my boyfriend's name on me,' you know, this and that—you know—'you think they'll do it for me?'—and I was like 'yeah.' 'Well what's up—let me go pick you up,' you know, 'can we go over there?'—and I was like—well 'F' it—I'm already—my mom's already tripping, so I mean—let's go. And so—they come to pick me up, and this is the first time I had—I had seen pictures of her on the internet with her boyfriend, but this is like the first time we meet. And my mom's like 'well—no, I don't want you going, you have school tomorrow,' you know,—this and this and that—'no, you're not gonna go,'—and I was like 'no, I *am* gonna go.' I was like 'I'll be right back.'—'oh Monica, don't go,'—'no, I *am* gonna go.'—'okay, okay, that's how you wanna play it—go ahead—go Monica,' and I said 'I'm going,'—so I took off…

Struggles over parental authority have not been modified from their pre-incarceration form. Monica's mother first attempts to exercise her authority with a direct command, 'no, you're not gonna go.' Monica dismisses her mother's command with 'no, I *am* gonna go,' to which her mother resorts to some semblance of a pleading—'oh Monica don't go.' After realizing that this battle was lost, Monica's mother resigns—'okay, okay, that's how you wanna play it—go ahead...'

Forms of Modification of Family Conflict— Navigating Compromises

Compromises are essential in modifying the dynamics of the insanity of place. There were some families in which conflict over parental authority was modified following release. This resulted in lessened tensions and a seemingly smoother post-release experience for the girls. This section will examine post-release experiences of those girls whose family authority conflicts were modified and explore some of the factors contributing to this modification.

Getting older, particularly reaching the age of 18, may alter the dimensions of family control struggles, thus easing post-release transition as a whole. If a girl reaches 18 while she is incarcerated, particularly if she has been incarcerated for a while, after she is released her parent is less likely to attempt to maintain the same restrictions over her actions as when she was a minor. Interestingly, in these instances, family control struggles are modified and although the girl may maintain many of the same behaviors she had prior to incarceration, now these behaviors are not a focus of control or conflict. The following passage in which Sabrina recounts her time spent away from home with her boyfriend illustrates how being 18 has modified her parent's attempt of restrictions placed on her time spent away from home:

> SABRINA: I used to sleep over there [boyfriend's]—I used to be over there... that's why I was never home.
> CARLA: So, you didn't argue with your mom about it, or anything?
> SABRINA: Uh-uh (negative). At first—when I first spent the night at his house—we used to argue about it. But I told her I'm grown. And she was like 'okay.'

CARLA: Okay, so you didn't really have a curfew or anything.

SABRINA: Uh-uh (negative). As long as I call her and check in. And let her know I'm okay... she didn't approve of it, but it was like—nothing she could do about it, cause I was like so in love with him—so into him.

Sabrina reveals that although initially her time spent away from home with her boyfriend caused friction between her and her mom (who was really her aunt), the conflict was seemingly resolved with Sabrina arguing that she was no longer a minor, or in her words—'I'm grown.' In this case it seems this may have served at least some basis for her mother/aunt backing down or easing her stance.

In those scenarios where the girls seem to have smoother post-release transitions, their family control struggles have been modified such that one or both parties have changed her stance in the struggle. Such a modification is illustrated in the following excerpt in which Rosa, who seems to be doing relatively well in comparison to the other girls, talks about how she is getting along with her family approximately six weeks after she was released:

ROSA: Everything's been cool. Like right now, I don't talk to no one in my house...my sister, I don't talk to her cause I'm just avoiding things. And that's how I would do it in [the facility], that's how I would do it. So that's what I'm doing—cause I know I'll just—get in a—fight with her. If I talk to her, cause I don't really like her— so I don't talk to her... my mom— she's sometimes not around so I don't really talk to—her. And when I do, it's just like 'oh god, mom—I'm doing good, trust me,' and like—

CARLA: She's really worried?

ROSA: Yeah. She don't give me no money—she don't give me money, like—if I wanna go out, like—she'll say 'nah—I'll go with you,' like if I wanna go buy something, she'll like 'I'll go with you, I'll go with you,' you know. I'm like 'ma, it's just right here, across the street,' and she's like 'nah, I'll go with you,' and I was like 'just give me the dol—' a *dollar*—she won't give it to me, she thinks I'll like start saving up money and then go and do drugs again—and like I don't blame her, I brought it up like, to myself, I thought it to myself, but still it's just—

CARLA: So how much freedom do you ha—how much—how much time can you be away from—them—I mean—do you really have to—like you can't do anything, go anywhere—

ROSA: I can't do anything. I can't do anything at all—the only freedom I have is when I'm at school.
CARLA: …so then you're pretty much—obeying what she says then.
ROSA: Yeah.

As this passage suggests reveals, Rosa's family reintegration does not seem to be marked with the degree of tumultuous conflict present in the other girls' experiences. This lack of conflict is in stark contrast to the struggle that existed before Rosa was incarcerated. The modification of this struggle seems to be at least partially the result of Rosa having accepted her mother's authority over her actions. From Rosa's comments about not really talking much to anyone in her family, it is not likely that this modification in family struggles resulted from an improvement in the quality of communications. She reveals that communication with her mom consists primarily of reassuring her mother that she is avoiding trouble. For whatever reason, Rosa seems to have at least for now accepted her mother's authority over her actions, which includes limiting her time away from home to school unless she allows her mother to accompany her. This is in stark contrast to her pre-incarceration habit of coming and going as she pleased in defiance to her mother's wishes:

CARLA: And so what keeps you from—okay, she's saying no, but…in the past…that didn't—really matter that much, you would still—maybe walk out and do it. So what keeps you from doing that?
ROSA: Back then—because I was on drugs so I didn't care. Now, I'm not on drugs and I see what could happen. You know, I don't wanna go to jail. I—don't wanna lose my family, even though I don't talk to them (laughing), but I don't wanna lose them. And—I just don't wanna go through that pain again cause I really felt lonely, you know, it's a depressing place to go to. And—I don't wanna go back—for myself—I don't wanna go back cause I'ma lose my family, if I lose my family—then they really don't love me and it's sad because they're family. But I don't wanna go back for myself, I don't wanna go back. So I just keep on thinking, you know, if you leave—at least—and you even come back early, if you leave without her permission—might as well just not come back. You know—that's how I think—if I ever—happen to like leave without her permission, I'm just not gonna come back. And I'm trying to avoid that.

Rosa reveals that the modification of family control struggles and her acceptance of the establishment or restoration of parental authority is in part the result of her being able to view things with the clarity afforded by sobriety. From this clarity of perspective, Rosa has a new concern with consequences of her actions. She sees the possibility of losing her family as a dire consequence of not accepting her mother's restrictions over her actions. This draws attention to the potential impact of drug use on family control struggles.

Sometimes there may be a conflict between the authority of the parent and the authority of the juvenile justice system. This is illustrated in the following scenario in which Rosa's mother's rules and restrictions conflict with those of Rosa's probation officer:

> ROSA: He's (probation officer) telling my mom, you know, 'it's okay for her to go out with her friends,' and like 'I know her curfew's at seven, but it's okay for her to come back at ten thirty, the latest, at ten thirty,'...and he's talked to her, he's told her, you know, 'it's okay for her to go out,' and my mom's like 'alright.' When it comes down to it, she w- she don't let me.

In this scenario, Rosa's mother's restrictions on her daughter's going out conflict with her formal probation curfew of 7:00 p.m., which her probation officer has extended until 10:30 p.m. Although Rosa's probation officer has talked with Rosa's mother, assuring her that it is acceptable not only to let Rosa go out, but to extend her curfew until 10:30 p.m., Rosa's mother rejects this advice, preferring to limit her daughter's time away from home only to school.

If a girl makes compromises with respect to parental authority by relinquishing autonomy, this may over time result in compromises being made by the parent. While in the beginning the trust level was low and Rosa's mother restricted her from going out, after six months, Rosa earned a degree of trust and her mother began letting her go out on Saturdays:

> ROSA: Since I started working with her, like she lets me go out...And she gives me money. So—before, she wouldn't give me money—she wouldn't let me go out.

CARLA: So, your relationship has improved-
ROSA: Yeah—it has improved a lot. Like we get along more.

Rosa compromised by relinquishing her autonomy and accepting her mother's authority. By accepting her mother's authority and adhering to her rules, Rosa contributed to the restoration of parental authority. In turn, over time, this resulted in compromises by the mother in granting some autonomy to Rosa.

While Rosa's post-release transition is characterized by a modification in family control struggles, which seems partly the result of Rosa accepting her mother's authority of her actions, Renee's post-release integration offers another view of how family control struggles might be modified. In Renee's case, family control struggles have largely dissipated partly as a result of Renee accepting her parents' authority but also because her parents have ceased attempting to establish authority in restricting Renee's action to the extent that they did in the past:

CARLA: How are you getting along with your—stepfather—with your father?
RENEE: It's—it's pretty cool. We haven't gotten into it. No arguments or anything. I—I—I—kinda stay out of his way—and he kinda stays out of mine—he usually takes me to school, so it's kinda like—(imitating a stern voice) 'get up.'—you know—and then like—'okay, bye. See you later,' or whatever—you know?—and—we really don't talk that much.

Control struggles have dissipated at least in part because she and her step-father have decided to keep their distance from each other. It seems that struggles have also dissipated between her and her mom:

RENEE: So, me and mom, we—we're cool or whatever—and—we—you know, we get into little—like—five seconds arguments, you know?—like—we disagree or whatever—but you know—that's like expected—it's nothing big—we don't—we haven't gotten into any fights or anything. So—things are cool—between me and my mom…she just gets on my nerves sometimes. But—she's been pretty flexible.

Renee further reveals that her mother does not have restrictions on where she goes during her times away from home, as long as she is home by her curfew of nine o'clock. She adds that on one occasion her mother has even extended curfew:

> CARLA: What time is your curfew?
> RENEE: …nine…like, my mom, she let me come home at—ten thirty when I went to R.'s (girl who was also released from the same facility) house…she extended it…I actually got home earlier than ten thirty. So, she was like 'oh—cool,'—like she could trust me or whatever.
> CARLA: …you don't really have any problem with….your mom telling you not to go out, or not to go anywhere?
> RENEE: As long as I'm home by nine…she's kinda trippin' off of me going to [city]—cause she knows I've been going to like—all the—like—in the middle of the hood—you know, like—in the ghetto and stuff.

These dynamics suggest how family control struggles have been modified in Renee's post-release transition. Renee now accepts some restrictions over her actions and her mother now allows her to go and does not question her whereabouts as long as she is home by her curfew time of nine o'clock. Another compromise that her mother makes is that she now lets Renee bring the guys that she meets to the house. This is significant because whereas before Renee was running away to meet or stay with guys, now she can bring them to the house which could mean that she is less likely to run away. In essence, this is a post-release circumstance in which the mother seems to make a lot of compromises, such as letting her daughter visit freely with friends both at her house and at their houses, and letting her bring boys home.

Since economic and racial/ethnic marginalization contributes to tensions running high, even if control struggles are modified between parent(s)/guardian and daughter, the girls may become involved in the power struggles of other family members. For example, they may become involved in their mother's power struggles with other members of the family. This is illustrated in the following exchange in which Mara goes to her mother's house (Mara lives with her grandmother) one day and becomes entangled in an argument taking place between her mother and her mother's boyfriend. The passage is necessarily long to illustrate the slow unfolding of how Mara is drawn into what she repeatedly attempts to avoid. It is a slow process in which the boyfriend publicly raises the question of her mother's character and respectability as a woman and mother. He introduces one charge after another against the mother: she is lazy; she is having sex with other men; she is a bad mother; and, finally, she is a drug addict. In essence, it is a form of public trial of humiliation intended to draw the support of the audience, who in this case is the daughter:

MARA: They musta been fighting for a couple days. I was like, I felt the vibe all of a sudden, and I was like 'oh *hell* no,' you know, I wanna get outa here. So—I was gonna leave, but I told my mom 'well, I need to leave,'... and she was like 'I don't want you leaving the house.' I was like 'alright, whatever'...and they were fighting for awhile, and I told my mom, 'you know what, I'm leaving,' and I started walking towards the back door...she was all 'no, I don't want you going to your grandma's house like *that*.' (Mara was high)...So I stayed...and they kept fighting...they really got at it and he blurted out loud, he was like 'yeah, that's why I found a condom in the toilet,'...and he started talking shit. So I was like—I was sitting there and I was letting most of it go. And he's all 'you don't know how to take care of your kids—you're out fucking around—you're out cheating,' he's like 'then you wonder why you don't have custody of any of your kids,' he was like 'cause you're always out fucking around.' And I was like '*kids?*' I was like—I—I fall in that category of kids, cause she doesn't have me either, so I'm like, who the fuck is he to talk shit to her? He's not nobody to judge my mom, you know, he's not perfect. And—so he was just talking shit to my mom...And he's like 'well, she has been, she's doing drugs again,...and—they're fighting. So all of a sudden, he pushes her into the wall—and I was gonna go at him, but my uncle came around me real quick—and he pushed him on the floor, he's like 'what the fuck is wrong with you [inaudible], don't be hitting my sister, what the hell's wrong with you?' and he ran outside, through the back, and he got a—um—crowbar or a pipe or something and he was hitting the house with it, and he was calling K. out...he's like 'come on K.,'...And the baby started crying, so she went into the room, and came back out into the dining room with the baby. And she's holding it, and they're *still* arguing. So—um—he lost his temper and pushed her again—not as hard—but he still pushed her into the *wall*, with the baby in her arms...and I pushed him, and he fell on the floor-...but he still pushed her again, that's when I went 'what the *fuck*, and

I pushed him and he fell on the floor,' I said 'what the fuck is wrong with you—that's a *female*,' I said 'you don't *never* hit a female—she ain't even touching you.' I said 'you're a bitch if you put your hands on a female and she ain't done nothing to you,' and he's all—he's all—'get the *fuck* outa my house,' and I was like—I was looking at him like, 'fuck you, you ain't nobody—that's my mom, you think I'ma sit here and defend you—I don't give a *fuck*,'...He got up *again*—and he looked at me, and he's all 'you know what, you're just like your mother,' *bam*—I socked him in his nose.

This exchange suggests how even with the best of intentions, the girls encounter power struggles on a daily basis that make them vulnerable to engaging in actions that may bring them in contact with the justice system. These structural circumstances shape the strategies that the girls use to navigate their everyday lives. These processes are such that in many instances, although the girls may try to exit or avoid these situations, they are drawn in. As this shows, Mara tries to exit the situation repeatedly; however, she is drawn in through a complex process involving her mother's pleas to stay and her mother's boyfriend's attempts to solicit Mara's support in the condemnation of her mother. The turning point is when the boyfriend accuses her mother of being a drug addict. This last discredit has particular significance for Mara because of her mother's drug addiction while Mara was a child, which is why Mara ended up living with her grandmother. The ultimate insult is when the boyfriend tells Mara that she is just like her mother. It is noteworthy that there is another adult man (Mara's uncle) present, but he retreats from the altercation leaving Mara and her mother to fend for themselves. Ultimately, Mara asserts her authority in the struggle in the only way assured to momentarily strip the boyfriend of his power. However, the boyfriend subsequently threatened to call the police, thus continuing the cycle of girls' involvement in domestic disputes being labeled as criminal acts.

Parental Authority: Threats, Bargaining Chips, and Money

If family control struggles resume after a girl is released, she may face the constant threat that her parent/guardian may report her 'misbehaviors' to the court or other authorities. The girls often fear that their freedom is dependent upon their parents:

MARA: My grandma—since we've been fighting, she's been threatening me, that she's gonna tell the—um—the court that I shouldn't be home... so I hope she doesn't do that. Because they'll put me right back in the system.

CARLA: So what's going on that your grandma's threatening to—say that you need to be back in?

MARA: Little things we'll argue over. Stupid little things, like I can't even think of them, that's how stupid they are. I don't even remember what we fight over. It starts off with something little, and then it works—very big. I don't know. But every *day*, there's a fight.

CARLA: Every day? So is that pretty much since you've been out—everyday? There's a fight?

MARA: No. More like a month after I got out. That's when it started...it's the—same thing all the time. And then she ends up picking up the phone, and I end up leaving the house. Cause I don't wanna stick around...to see the cops if she does call 'em.

The grandmother's leverage in their arguments consists of constant threats to report Mara to either the police or court officials at her upcoming hearing. It is debatable whether this is an effective tool to bring her granddaughter in line, but it is enough to keep Mara in a heightened state of anxiety.

Similarly, the following passage also illustrates how after the girls are released, their parent (generally mother or grandmother) often presents more of a threat to their continuing freedom than do their probation officers:

CARLA: Okay, so your mom hasn't done any calling the cops, right?

CATHY: No. She threatens me all the time—she threatens to call—my P.O...it's basically my mom. Cause my P.O.—you know—everything's cool with her. It's just my mom.

CARLA: So, your P.O. knows about your promoting [employment as a club promoter]—and your—and that?

CATHY: No—she can't know. I'll get violated for that.

Although Cathy was violating her probation terms, including her curfew and not going to school, her probation officer wrote a glowing report and

Cathy's judge said she did not have to come back to court anymore until her probation was terminated.

The constant fear that their parent (or guardian) may turn them in takes on additional dimensions when the girl has an independent source of income and there is an exchange of money for the parent's silence. Elements of such a scenario are suggested in the following passage as Cathy discusses her relationship with her mom after her release. Tensions began almost immediately, a few days after release:

> CATHY: We don't get along—my mom and me—we're not getting along at all...not just that, but a lot of stuff—she wants me to—give her money—she's always breaking off some money—like—I let her borrow eighty bucks one time, she didn't pay me back. She asks me for money for this and that—like yesterday, I gave her twenty dollars, and stuff and so on...she tries to manipulate me, saying, you know, well this and this and this—for money—so she'll be quiet—and not tell my P.O...my mom—like if she snitches on me, I'ma be violated—you know what I mean?—and—I gotta make sure, so I have to kinda let her manipulate me—break her off [money]—but I don't know—it's not working—cause I give her money, then she manipulates me for more—like the next minute. She—she just wants—she wants all the money—everything—and I can't be doing that... Cause she wants me doing too much—you know?—*too* much—and it's like it's not gonna work that way—she's gonna manipulate me—take my *money*.

Cathy, age 17, works as a club promoter, which means that she works nights, rendering adherence to a probation curfew virtually impossible. Although this constitutes employment and an earned source of income, it places Cathy in the very same environment from which she is supposed to be working to get away—the club scene. Cathy has found a way to make money while doing what she loves to do most—hanging out in clubs. Additionally, she is not attending school; however, she and her mother have an unspoken agreement that her mother will keep her silence in exchange for some of Cathy's money earned in this job.

Earning an income or making money is one way that the girls may increase their autonomy after they are released. Since their status as minors may limit both their options for employment and their income potential, some of them may bypass this by becoming involved in more prosperous ventures generally occupied by adults. This is the case of Cathy's job as a club promoter. The following suggests Cathy's recognition that perhaps this is not an appropriate job for her and how she rationalizes her preference for this type of work:

> CATHY: About the promoting—I ended up doing it—I'm probably gonna get out cause it's kinda dangerous…It's scary sometimes, cause I meet weird people and—it's just—scary—and I have to deal with a lot of people, like 'oh, I'm gonna be there tonight,'—you know, I have to flirt sometimes and do all kinds of stuff. But, I mean—just on Friday nights—Saturday— but—I don't go every week—and—but I promote—when I have to promote, I have to go everywhere—like I go to—lounges—you know—like the hotel lounges—like downstairs—talk to people—meet people—tell 'em about the club…I—I mean I wanna get out—it's just the money's so addictive, Carla. Oh my god, it is. It's like I never have—I always have money—like right now, I have like $500 bucks in my purse. That's how good…I've just seen this money be so good that—it's just *quick*.

Accepting money from their daughters undoubtedly complicates struggles over parental authority in the long run. It was not uncommon for mothers at some point to accept money from their daughters. Clearly, parental authority is jeopardized when a parent relies on a daughter's money to pay for basic necessities for the family. One of the most basic socially expected responsibilities of a parent is to financially provide basic necessities for the family; thus, it is difficult to accept the role of a dependent child in need of supervision and guidance from a parent who is having trouble fulfilling this expected responsibility.

Navigating Other Challenges of Everyday Life

Returning to their families after release is enormously stressful for the girls as they are left to navigate contentious family and other relations with no support systems. Whether and how the girls are able to cope with these challenges are key factors shaping whether the girls are able to sever ties with the juvenile justice system. Navigating contentious family relations is intertwined with a myriad of other challenges the girls have to navigate. While it is not within the scope of this section to examine in any depth the myriad of challenges encountered by the girls, this section will briefly suggest some of the types of challenges that the girls encounter that are compounded by family power struggles.

The stresses and strains of the girls' lives intertwined with their family conflicts make them susceptible to drug use and other relapses. For example, in the following passage, Rosa tells of how her family's inattention to her birthday results in a near drug use relapse as well as a near runaway relapse:

> ROSA: I was gonna get—tweak. I was gonna go do a line or something with someone. I didn't know who. Cause I was at home and it was night time, I was just gonna leave and I wasn't gonna come back. Cause it was for my birthday. Cause on Sat—Saturday was my birthday. I didn't get nothing. I didn't get nothing—that's—that's what's on my mind right now like—a lot—because I didn't get nothing—it hurt me a lot because—it was—it was sad, no one—I wasn't like 'oh you guys have to give me something,' you know, I didn't say anything about it, but it hurt me a lot that they didn't like—my brother didn't say happy birthday to me.
> CARLA: Did they forget?
> ROSA: *No.* My mom said happy birthday to me and my best friend came over with a cake. That's all I got…I stayed up all night—like I didn't take my medicine, so I stayed up all night, and I was like—whatever, you know, I'm—I'm—I'm leaving tomorrow, I'm not gonna come back, I'm leaving, I'm leaving and—I didn't sleep—it was—it was—I was crying, I was like—oh whatever, you know, I guess they don't love me (chuckle). So I was just real sad for my birthday—it wasn't—it wasn't what I expected, I expected at least *one* present from my mom. She didn't give me nothing. She didn't give me nothing. So, I was like—my birthday's [inaudible], you know. So—that's what made me relapse and then—it didn't make me—because I didn't do it, but it was making me want to.

This gives a sense of the fragility of the girls' lives and how the circumstances of their lives are such that even when they seem to be doing relatively well, they are often on the brink of slipping. Since most of the girls are prone to depression (largely shaped by the circumstances of their lives), during any disappointments, they will be more susceptible to relapses. It could happen any minute through a myriad of precipitating events.

Because most of the girls do not have support systems with whom they can express their emotions, they often use mechanisms other than verbal communication in an attempt to release these emotions, particularly anger and pain or suffering. One common method used by girls in the juvenile justice system is 'cutting.' Cutting is an act in which a girl uses a sharp device, such as a razor blade, to make tiny cuts on some place on her body, usually somewhere on the arm. In the following passage, Miranda reveals that she has been 'cutting' since her release:

MIRANDA: See all them little white scars.

CARLA: Yeah…Okay, so tell me about that—what happened and why did you do it?—what were you thinking?

MIRANDA: A mood swing—the depression and I was just—thinking about all this shit—I don't know.

CARLA: Where were you?

MIRANDA: Here (her home).

CARLA: You were by yourself?

MIRANDA: *Um-hm(affirmative)*—I get—I don't know—for some reason, when I'm chillin' with my friends, I'll be cool—but I'll step in this house—and like—I'll just see certain little things, and I'll think—and I'll just get mad and irritated—like—uuh. Can't fuckin' stand *livin* here…And I'll just get real mad. Just—uhh…and then I get mad thinking about my mom—I can not *stand* my mom at all.

CARLA: What is it about her?—*Why* can't you stand her?

MIRANDA: She's a fuckin' *idiot.*

CARLA: *Why* do you think that?

MIRANDA: She acts stupid—she say stupid stuff—she do stupid things…

CARLA: So, that'll get you mad—what other kind of things? It gets you mad—and depressed, or-

MIRANDA: No, not depressed, it just gets me *mad*—as hell…All I know is that I cut myself—felt physical pain and was straight—took my [inaudible] down to D.D.'s house. Smoked me a blunt to calm my ass down and was cool.

CARLA: Oh, okay, so you were sober when you cut—when you did that—what'd you cut it with?

MIRANDA: Razor blade.
CARLA: Just on the one arm? Okay, so you—you did it on both or one?
MIRANDA: Both.

Cutting is sometimes misunderstood by those in the mental health profession and misinterpreted as a sign of attempted suicide. However, the girls talk about 'cutting' in terms of the release it provides and in terms of relieving pain:

ROSA: When you cut yourself, when you're cutting yourself, it's like a relief like—you just get everything out cause you're so mad—so you cut yourself and you see the pain and all that and it relieves your pain. And the—drugs - does the same thing, you know, it gets you out of—reality. And that's what cutting—does to you. Well, that's how I see it—that's how most people see it.
CARLA: But what about the fact that each time you cut, it hurts? It's causing you pain, though.
ROSA: I don't know what it—I don't know. Like it r— like— I'll be really frustrated, I'll be really depressed, I'll be like really hurting—because—something happened in the family, or whatever—or things are not going my way and I'll go and cut myself, I'll just be—relaxed—I'll be like (exhaling). Like everything's okay now.
CARLA: And you don't feel the pain? You feel the pain?
ROSA: You don't—*I* don't feel it. I don't feel it—I just—[inaudible]
CARLA: What do you cut with?
ROSA: A razor.
CARLA: And so, you don't really feel—you don't feel it?
ROSA: Cause it's so sharp that you don't even feel it. You don't even—like—it just—just slides in you—you see all the blood gushing out, but I mean—to me—like—for most people, they really don't feel it. They really don't feel it—because you're so mad that you don't feel anything. You're so depressed that you don't even—whatever emotion you have that—is—causing—all this pain—that once you cut yourself, you don't feel it at all. And then it's just a relief—you feel much better—like—your heart stops and you're like (exhaling) you can breathe again. That's—that's how it is with me, I don't know if it's like that for others, but—that's how it is with me—and like—I don't wanna do it, but I've been doing it for so long that it's like ad - like it's an addiction. It's like drugs, so...it's mostly when I'm

mad…and—when—I don't get my way or when I'm like I'm trying to—tell you something and you're not listening to what I'm trying to tell you, that's when I—do it.

Given the emotional stressors of post-release, it was not uncommon for the girls to fondly recall more seemingly carefree times while incarcerated:

CARLA: You were saying earlier that sometimes you wish you were back there. At [the facility]. Tell me about that.

MARA: I don't know because there's—I had my good moments in [the facility] where like—where we'll just *laugh*. Like me and—me and Ms. S. and Maria would just have times where—me and Maria and Sabrina used to just play around and—push each other on the wall—remember we used to do that? And I'll just think about that, the things we do down the halls, and—me and Maria used to talk through the walls, you know—just little things that we're not supposed to do that we do. And it's like it's no big deal. But—and you come out here and you try and do things like—you can't do things like that—[inaudible], but you try and do little things wrong, it's a big thing. It's like fuck nah—let the little shit go, but they don't. And I miss Ms. S.—a lot. I miss her so much. Like last night—I was crying because I was remembering the day she took me out to go get my clothes—she took me shopping because I needed to go get my clothes, and I didn't have a ride—

CARLA: This was after you got out?

MARA: Yeah. It was like a week after, maybe…I was crying so hard last night because I miss her.

While it may seem ironic for someone to reminisce fondly about her moments of incarceration, the fact that Mara does so suggests the degree of difficulty and the depth of despair felt by many of the girls after their release. It suggests that even with the abolition of freedoms entailed in incarceration, it provides a sense of stability, certainty, and levity absent from the lives of these girls on the outside. It is not uncommon for girls to say that the thing that they miss about being in the facility is that while incarcerated there, they did not have to worry about anything. This is in no way suggesting any humaneness or civility about incarceration, but rather a comment on the chaos, instability, and severity that distinguishes the girls' lives on the outside.

No doubt that the difficulties of post-release are stressful not only for the daughters, but for their parents as well. The following field note excerpt from my conversation with Mara's grandmother suggests the tension felt from the parent/grandparent's viewpoint:

Mara's grandmother said 'She's not doing well…' About three quarters of the way into the conversation, she mentioned that Mara's response is always 'I'm following the rules.' Her grandmother continued by confirming that Mara follows the rules, saying she goes to school and is always home by 6:00 p.m. Mara's grandmother said the problem is Mara's temper. She said that Mara needed help, psychological help, some kind of counseling because 'she has so much anger in her.' She said she didn't want to tell Mara's P.O. because she did not want to get Mara in trouble, didn't want her to be locked up again…At one point, she said 'I mean she has changed *some*.'…Mara's grandmother said that Mara hangs around with three friends whom she (the grandmother) does not like, but that her main concern is that Mara has so much anger in her—has such a temper…Mara's grandmother said that Mara's grandfather did not want Mara there, saying 'He doesn't want her here anymore. But what can I do—I can't put her out—and I don't want her locked up again—she was in there so long last time—she was in there two years—I don't understand why she was in there locked up for so long.'

We not only get a sense of the frustration of the grandmother, but also gain insight on other salient issues as well. We learn that Mara's keen concerns that her grandmother will report to the court that she is not doing well (as noted in interview excerpts above) are unfounded. On the contrary, it seems that this is the last thing that her grandmother wants to do as she states above that she does not want to tell Mara's probation officer because she does not want to get Mara in trouble—does not want her to be locked up again. With this, Mara's grandmother conveys her sense of helplessness by asking what she can do. She realizes her options are limited, as she briefly considers them—'I can't put her out—and I don't want her locked up again.' While she once was in favor of using the justice system to assist with imposing discipline, she now is reluctant to use this recourse. In her view, it did nothing to improve the circumstances and resulted in a much longer incarceration time than she had anticipated. The lack of perceived options open to the grandmother was underscored by her appealing to me about whether I knew of anything—any programs that might help her granddaughter. She suggested this was not something that she would have addressed with the probation officer even if he had been involved for fear she might get Mara in trouble or incarcerated again. Mara's grandmother's fears of contacting Mara's probation officer highlights the problematic nature of a system that combines punitive and therapeutic functions under one umbrella. The girls and their families never get the help that they need because revealing their problems and fallacies places the girls at risk for further detainment or closer supervision.

Lastly, Mara's grandmother's comments, as well as other narratives in this section, suggest that measuring a girl's post-release experiences by whether she is following probation rules may not be the best measure of post-release 'success.' This is illustrated by the fact that although the main theme that Mara's grandmother conveys to me during our conversation is that Mara is not doing well, about three quarters of the way into the conversation, she casually mentions that Mara does follow the probation rules—she goes to school every day and is always home by 6:00 p.m. This was ironic because many, including Mara's probation officer, considered the fact that she was following probation rules to be an indicator that Mara was 'doing well.'

Discussion and Conclusion

Most post-release studies focus on the experiences of adults. Previous studies of post-release experiences of adult prisoners suggest a process of major readjustment that would tax the strengths of most persons. For the most part, the context of reintegration differs for adolescent girls. First, although there may be some girls who have been incarcerated for longer terms, the girls have primarily been incarcerated for relatively short terms; thus, being on the outside again is generally not the shock to the system that it is for some of their older counterparts. Additionally, while adult prisoners face the daunting challenge of obtaining gainful employment, for most adolescent girls, this is not an immediate necessity. However, this is not to suggest that reintegration for adolescent girls is an easier task. Because of their status as juveniles, the girls face some difficult circumstances not faced by their older counterparts. Since periods of incarceration are unlikely to contribute to improving the family control struggles that propelled the girls into the system, after the girls are released, these control struggles are one of the most difficult challenges with which they must contend.

Since family control struggles facilitate girls' entry into the system and the girls return to these same power struggles, programming should include developing community resources to help mediate these conflicts. This would provide parents with an alternative to involving the cops in mediating family conflicts. Any program that does not also address the needs of the families, particularly the mothers, or other woman guardians, will fall woefully short because this is to whom the girls return. Instead of directing resources toward building programs within institutions, the girls and their families would be better served by emphasizing and developing community programs, rather than institutional programs.

Given that family power struggles are a significant factor in the girls' lives, including bringing them in contact with the justice system, one possible resource would be some form of community conflict mediation entity to help diffuse conflicts. Of the girls in the study, only Renee had an aftercare program whose function served to impact family control struggles. While it is only one program, it provides some points of consideration for informing how such a resource might work and what improvements might be made for development of similarly situated programs. There are two ways that such a program may help diffuse family conflict: by serving as an alternate form of parental authority under a seemingly less-threatening guise; and by serving as a support network to girls, as well as their parent(s).

RENEE: They always call me—'oh, how are you doing?'…they're always bugging me. And that's what they are—they're supposed to do…make sure I'm—I'm focused, and I'm—out of trouble and everything, so…they're very—persistent with me, and—always on top of things—'oh—we have an appointment here—do you remember that?—oh, I'm gonna pick you up from school today, and we're gonna—go look for—a job,' or whatever…the main goal—to help me—is to get off probation—that's their goal…They—we have a meeting every other week—at my house—they come—all of 'em—and we talk about me—and my life—and how we can improve things—and our topics that we usually talk about is just friends, job, and school…There's a team of—well—four people now—but it's—it's usually three…there's three people on the team—right?—but one of 'em is—is for me, the other one is for my parents, and—the other one is just like—to help out with both—you know what I mean?—so the one lady that's assigned to me…she takes me out sometimes…the very first time we went out, she took me out to lunch…second time, we went to this—like job search place—where you put in like a application and they call you… usually she comes over too and we'll like have—I'll make something, like at home—like—throw something in the oven, and—we'll eat at my house or something…she's like in her—twenties or something.

In this model, Renee's aftercare program consists of a team of three people whose purpose is to monitor her progress as closely as possible to ensure that she gets off of probation. The members of the team are divided such that one serves as primary support for Renee, one serves as primary support for her parents, and the third member provides a neutral form of support. Although there is a support person provided to the parents, Renee's stepfather is not involved and leaves this to Renee's mother to navigate. This is continuation of the pattern that even when men are present, they remove themselves from the power struggles such that they are primarily between women. The support network that constitutes aftercare is especially critical since the probationary period is a time of heightened vulnerability since the girls can be re-incarcerated for violating even the simplest probation rules. This arrangement has the potential to diffuse family conflict in that it functions as a non-parent entity exercising control functions while simultaneously acting, or at least appearing to act, as an advocate for the girls' autonomy.

However, although an aftercare program or entity might diffuse power struggles between a parent and daughter, it simultaneously creates new power struggles for the girls to navigate—between the daughter and the support person(s) of the aftercare program. One of the sources of contention between Renee and the aftercare program representative(s) is over their encouraging—or in Renee's words—'pushing' her to get a job. Getting a job was not a previous source for contention in the family control struggles as this was not on her parents' agenda. Eventually, Renee asserts her autonomy on the issue of finding a job, and the program representative compromises (or concedes) and ceases the push for Renee to get a job:

> CARLA: What about this job thing—last time, they were all geared into getting you this job—and to get these applications—what happened with that?
> RENEE: ….I just—I said screw you—I don't want a job, so I'm not doing it—and I stuck to my guns with that—or whatever—and um—she's like 'hey—fine,'—or whatever—cause she was really pushing me—really—and it was really bugging me, like how is she gonna make me get a job?—you know what I mean?—there's not—um—like probation things to get a job—and I'm like 'no, I don't want a job,'—you know what I mean?—I'm not ready to work—you know?…. I'm just like 'uh-uh,'—and I just—no—you know?—and just stuck to it—so she hasn't been pressuring me about a job lately. Yeah—she kinda—backed off with the job thing…I really don't want a job right now…I don't want to work—I just want to hurry up and finish school.

The 'Insanity of Place' framework in chapter three may be applied to any arrangement in which one party asserts authority or makes demands for change in an attempt to elevate his/her status. The twist is that while in family negotiations of this circumstance, the parent does not generally have the option of removing herself from the situation, the aftercare authority does have that option, and this is precisely what happened. There were disagreements over finding a job, as well as Renee's frequent talking about the men in her life. Consequently, the representative who was working with Renee withdrew from the arrangement, and the program brought in someone else:

RENEE: And then she used to complain cause I used to talk about guys all the time, or my boyfriends, and—she used to be like 'god Renee—can't you talk about something else?'—I'm like 'fuck you,'—you know?—this is my—you know—you're—pshh—if it wasn't for me, you wouldn't—you know?—like—you—pshh—I'm on—you're—you have my case—you know?—so I'm like I'ma talk about what I wanna talk about—but whatever—I didn't tell her that, but I'm—you know?—that's what I'm thinking. But whatever—so, she got assigned to another case, because um—this new lady—came in, and so like—it kinda worked out—that girl B.—and I've only known her for like two, three weeks—and she is so cool—I can open up and tell her, like anything…she like—helps me, like at my pace—you know?—like—what I wanna do and stuff—we're gonna go shopping next week—so—I'm all happy—I'm gonna go shopping.

That the aftercare program produces new power struggles is to be expected since power struggles and surveillance are inevitable components of all institutional arrangements. The aftercare program is in the same precarious position as other support entities such as the institutional therapists who are simultaneously probation officers. Since aftercare representatives share information with probation officers (e.g., Renee's probation officer is usually at every aftercare meeting), they are, in effect, an extension of the justice system's surveillance. However, the P.O. and the aftercare representative had differerent goals and different styles of governing. The P.O. was more lenient and focused on Renee's finishing school. The aftercare program was stricter and focused on more long term goals. This was particularly salient when, as in Renee's case, there were differences in opinion between the aftercare program and her P.O. as to when Renee's probation should be terminated. The aftercare representative was in favor of a longer period of probation than her P.O. thought necessary:

CARLA: Was Mr. D. (her P.O.)—he um—he usually—how often does he come to the meetings with the [aftercare] people?
RENEE: Usually every time.

CARLA: Oh, really? So, [aftercare] is a kind of thing where—they, like—I mean do you feel that you can—tell [aftercare] people stuff and have it not get back to your P.O.? Or you pretty much know—like whatever you tell them-
RENEE: ...everything—that I tell her—goes back to Mr. D... she told him that um—because I—I'm like—'you know what?—I don't even wanna be here anymore,'—because this is like how bad I was feeling—I'm like 'I wanna go back to placement—where I don't have to deal with anything, and everything's done for me, and I could just kick back and just get through school and not worry about anything,'—you know?—I'm like 'I have too much stuff to worry about—I'm stressed out—I don't wanna worry about all this shit anymore,'—and then I'm like 'I wanna go back somewhere—I wanna go—just until I get out of school, and then I can think about what I need to do and-'—I'm like, 'but until then—I don't wanna deal with this crap anymore,'—I hate being out here—I'm like—da-da-da-da-da—and she went back and told him all that...and he's like 'I have my money on you,'—he's like 'you're like the only one who's made it,'—you know?—like—this far—hasn't messed up or anything—he's like 'I don't have to violate you for anything,'—he's like 'you don't have any problems,'...little does he know.

An aftercare program is not just an extension of surveillance for the girls, but for the parent(s) or guardians as well; thus families are not keen about aftercare either. However, this is not to suggest that the concept of an aftercare program should be dismissed; rather, it points to the need to carefully craft community programs that are not simply extensions of the justice system. Since family control struggles facilitate girls' entry into the system and the girls return to these same struggles, the girls and their families would be better served by developing community, rather than institutional, programs. This would provide parents or guardians with an alternative to involving the police in mediating family conflicts. Any program that does not also address the needs of the families, particularly the mothers or other woman guardians, will fall woefully short because this is the primary context of the power struggles.

Reference

Hurtado, Aida. 1996. *The Color of Privilege*. Ann Arbor: University of Michigan Press.

6

Navigating Neighborhood Institutions: Gang Involvement

MONICA: me and C., stopped getting along because—I felt like she was ta—it was so awkward because—we were fighting for the stupidest reason—I felt like she was taking my place—like they were showing her a lot of attention and this and that—but she was getting attention from the little guys. The big guys—would never—you know—they didn't trust her like they trusted me—so, I—you know—I still thought I was the shit. And they had me so manipulated—that I thought—I was running—because you know I was the only girl ever allowed to—to roll with them cars—I was the only girl—to count money for them—to—you know—to do *everything*—I was the only girl allowed in the houses. I thought I had moved up in the world...I just thought I was on top of the world, you know—oh my God—these—these main guys respect me and they trust me and—and this is what I always wanted...

Family control struggles are not the only forces shaping the girls' lives. As mentioned in previous chapters, families are shaped by their positions in the larger socio-economic context. Socio-economic marginalization fractures bonds and fosters a sense of alienation in the family, which makes the girls more vulnerable to gaining a primary sense of worth through

© The Author(s) 2017
C.P. Davis, *Girls and Juvenile Justice*,
DOI 10.1007/978-3-319-42845-1_6

other institutions. Within this context of alienation, gang involvement has heightened appeal to the girls. There are no alternative institutions offering a comparable sense of validation. Although the girls occupy low status in these organizations, they construct their identities in such a way as to accord themselves a sense of worth. As indicated by the above narrative, the girls derive a sense of status through rationalizing being one of the few (or only) girls as an indicator of their worth.

On the surface, it appears that guys in the gang have deemed the girls trustworthy members of a group (girls) otherwise deemed to be untrustworthy. However, notions of the untrustworthiness of members of devalued groups have a context in simultaneous intersecting structures of race/ethnicity, gender, as well as class. Slavery shaped the historical dual construction of womanhood and consequent dominant ideas of the moral superiority of White women. Thus, these processes may also be seen as the girls' attempts to distance themselves from the stigma of being Black and Brown girls. Certainly, dominant ideas of women's lack of rationality (i.e., questions concerning the capacity for sound judgment) serve as a basis for discrediting all women's trustworthiness. However, dominant ideas of White women's moral superiority at least affords them the benefit of the doubt—they are less likely to *automatically* be deemed untrustworthy.

Distancing themselves from the stigma of being Black and Brown girls is a way for the girls to compete for place—or status—as the 'chosen one' in a world in which they occupy a devalued status by virtue of being at the bottom of the hierarchical structure. This chapter examines how the girls distance themselves from the stigma of being Black and Brown girls in competing for status in their gang associations. It explores how the girls rationalize being 'chosen' as an indicator that they are different from (morally superior to) the 'typical' member of their devalued group. The girls' narratives reveal the contradictions between the girls' sense of status and their actual status. Regardless of their feelings of status, by making sense of their gang involvement as being the 'chosen one,' the girls are reproducing structures of inequality. However, even if their actual circumstances contradict their illusions, their illusions are significant because they form the basis for the girls' actions.

Status as a Neglected or Misinterpreted Framework for Studying Girls and Gangs

As suggested in chapter one, a by-product of previous studies' conceptualizing gender as an individual attribute is the scarcity of research using attainment of status as a primary framework. Previous studies struggle to articulate how aspects of identity are connected to a larger system of resources, status, and power. Studies that attempt to link material conditions to girls' identity construction and actions tend to treat status in one of two ways: they either underestimate the significance of status or interpret status in a way that posits gender as a dichotomously constructed individual attribute expressing universal essential differences between men and women. For example, the finding that boys join gangs to gain status, while girls join gangs out of fear, loneliness, and a need to connect (Campbell 1993). Interestingly, this reflects sentiments of earlier scholars, such as Morris (1964), attempting to apply strain theory to understanding girls' delinquency.

Studies attempting to link girls' gang associations with status conceptualize race, gender, class as individual attributes comprising 'doing gender,' rather than as overarching, simultaneous operating structures. For example, although (1995) places her study in a larger material context and acknowledges the relevance of status for girls in gangs, she posits it in terms of girls assuming masculine characteristics and thus becoming empowered. She says that girls join gangs to learn how to fight and hustle, thereby better preparing them to become independent women. In this view, attaining power and status is predicated on deviance to gender roles reflected in stereotypical notions of masculinity or femininity. Once again, gender is conceptualized as an individual attribute rather than a structure comprising the distribution of resources, status, and power. Similarly, Harris (1997) notes status as a reason for girls belonging to gangs, but narrowly links status to the girls' engagement in risk-taking activities embodying stereotypical gender norms. Also, previous studies that consider status do not distinguish the difference between actual status in the gang and the girls' sense or perceptions of status. As girls in a male-dominated structure, their actual status differs from their subjective sense of status in these affiliations.

While later studies of girls and gangs acknowledge the relevance of status, there is still a scarcity of studies applying status as a primary framework. For example, Valdez (2007) suggested that 'low income neighborhood young females may be attracted to male gang members because of the status associated with their membership'; however, he does not examine this dimension and how it connects to the girls' constructions of identity, position in the hierarchical structure, as well as subsequent actions. Similarly, while Miller (2001) briefly notes that a route to status for girls in the gang was via their connection to influential males in the gang, she does not make the phenomenon of status a central framework. She does not examine the processes of connections between status, the girls' constructions of self, perceptions of their surrounding circumstances, and how this translates into the various ways that they navigate gang affiliations. Also, as Chesney-Lind (2014) suggests, Miller seems to view status as linked to race and class oppression but not necessarily to gender hierarchies. Again, this reflects a struggle to conceptualize race, gender, class as simultaneous intersecting structures as well as a struggle to conceptualize how macro and micro processes are linked. As a result, Miller offers a literal accounting of the girls' words and actions rather than placing them in a larger context of meanings to offer an overarching theory for the girls' actions.

It is ironic that Cambell (1993) does not make a connection between status attainment and girls' associations with gangs considering that one of her previous studies examined processes of identity formation of ethnically marginalized girls in gangs. In her investigation of girls in a gang in New York (1990), Campbell suggests that gang girls cope with their social location of being poor Puerto Rican girls by rejecting aspects of themselves associated with that social position. In other words, they attempt to distance themselves from the stigma of being Puerto Rican girls. This is manifested through their talk, in which they take those parts of themselves that they reject and use them to criticize and sanction other girls' actions and characters. They draw boundaries between themselves and other girls, simultaneously constructing themselves as not being like the objects of vilification. Campbell suggests that closer examination of gossip and other forms of 'put-downs' can illuminate how identity is constructed. However, while Campbell notes the processes of distancing as an important component of identity construction, she does not examine how the rejection of aspects of self is connected to a larger system of power and status.

Failure to place identity construction of girls in the juvenile system in a larger context of a system of power and status reflects the failure to do so in literature on gendering processes in general. For example, while previous studies (Carr 1998; Hollander 2002; Silva 2008) have noted the phenomenon of women differentiating themselves from other women, these studies view gender primarily as something embedded in performance. These performances are viewed in the context of 'doing gender,' and the alleged empowerment gained from using individual agency to subvert norms. They fail to consider how these actions appearing to subvert the power structure actually reinforce gender, race/ethnicity, and class hierarchies, as well as reinforce the individual performer's status at the bottom. Brown's (2003) study of adolescent girls is an exception to this general failure. Brown notes the centrality of competition for status in the construction of identity/selves and lives of girls from an early age. However, she fails to consider the intersecting larger structure of race/ethnicity in the construction of girls' identities. Considering how gender intersects with race/ethnicity is important in understanding how systems of oppression affect women at different race/ethnic locations in the hierarchical structure. As Hurtado (1996) and others note, White women do not experience oppression similarly to women of color. Because of the dual construction of womanhood, White women are oppressed with a dimension of respect not accorded to women of color. Further, unlike women of color, White women are at least accorded a significant opportunity to share in the *fruits* of power and status through their connections (as wives, daughters, sisters, girlfriends, etc.) to the group who holds power. In essence, unlike women of color, White women have the opportunity to raise their status through their connections to the group in power.

Ultimately, previous studies fall short of exploring the links between material conditions of simultaneous race/ethnic, gender, class oppression and processes of in how girls in the justice system navigate their lives. By contrast, this chapter asks: *what is the connection between material conditions of multiple levels of social marginalization and negotiation of identity, status, and power in shaping girls' gang associations?* It places the attainment of status in the larger context of gender, race/ethnicity, and class as larger simultaneous systems of resources, status, and power rather than individual attributes. The data illustrate how the girls gain a sense of worth from being the only or one of a few members from their devalued group. They make sense of this phenomenon as an indicator that they were chosen because they are trustworthy, thus different from the 'typical' member of their devalued group. This chapter will examine the ways the girls draw upon ideals of citizenship to make sense of being the chosen one in ways to accord them at least a sense of status.

Ways of Rationalizing Being the Chosen One

The Homegirl or 'One of the Guys'

How a girl draws upon dominant ideals to make sense of being one of a few or the only girl depends upon her mode of incorporation. In other words, it depends on how she is integrated into the social structure of the gang. The term mode of incorporation is commonly reserved for literature on race/ethnic and immigrant stratification. It refers to how racial, ethnic, or immigrant groups are initially incorporated into a society. The initial mode of incorporation is significant because it greatly shapes access to resources, status, and power for initial, as well as subsequent, generations of that group. There are different ways in which the girls can be integrated into gang structure. These varying ways of integration are tantamount to modes of incorporation, reflected in varied social locations, such as that of homegirl, hoodrat, girlfriend, and so on. I use the term mode of incorporation to reflect these as institutional processes rather than static categories. Each mode of incorporation simultaneously reflects and shapes how the girls make sense of self and circumstances and how they navigate these circumstances.

No matter the mode of incorporation, the girls all draw upon a mixture of ideals of worker-citizen and ideal womanhood. However, a girl's particular mode of incorporation shapes the ways that she mixes these dominant ideals to construct herself in a way that accords her a sense of status. In some ways, these different ways of drawing upon ideals of citizenship reflect Brown's (2003) sentiments on the ways or options that girls have in competing for status in the social world. Brown writes, '…to be female in a culture so invested in boys and girls being different, while at the same time privileging qualities associated with maleness, offers a girl limited options…she can identify with boys—be one of the guys—or she can act in ways that boys find pleasing and desirable. If she's clever, she can do both' (30). Of course gender intersects with structures of race/ethnicity to constrain the extent to which girls of color can do either—let alone both.

The mode of incorporation most commonly reflected in the scholarly literature on girls and gangs is that of the 'homegirl' or 'one of the guys.' This is somewhat ironic considering that many girls associated with gangs fall outside this mode of incorporation. While previous literature studies homegirls, there has been an absence of data examining their social locations in the hierarchical structure, how that shapes construction of their identities, and how it shapes the strategies they employ to navigate their lives. Previous studies of girls incorporated in the mode of homegirl tend to focus on girls' gang activities in the context of violence, suggesting that girls gain some sense of empowerment through engaging in these acts of violence. However, focusing on girls and gangs in the context of violence reflects a very small segment of girls' associations with gangs and ignores the larger context of girls' involvement. In a larger structural context, the narratives of those incorporated as homegirls reveal that they gain a sense of status from feeling that they are valued and respected for their work contributions:

> GLORIA: I used to carry—like drugs and stuff for my homeboys—like— *all* through the night—like—okay, let's—I would be sleeping in my house, right? And like—well, pretending to sleep. And so like—my mom—everybody would be sleeping, and I would sneak out late at night…So, I'm walking with like—all kind of dope on me and shit all the time—you know, I would stick it up my—you know—private part and—all kinds of private parts—you know?…And they trust me for some reason—they trusted me—you know? It was always Crystal Meth…my whole—my whole job was—transportation…Basically. To get it from here to there…

Homegirls gain a sense of status through their contributions as workers, and their work contributions are varied. However, as suggested above, it is not so much the work in itself that gives the sense of value as much as the sense that they are *trusted* in doing the work and that this in itself distinguishes them from other women. The girls derive status from a sense that they are trusted members of a group otherwise deemed untrustworthy:

> CARLA: …tell me what it's like to be in a gang…tell me why you like it.
> ALICE: I like—I don't know—like—I—I like—I like hanging around with boys—cause they're not like backstabbers like girls.
> CARLA: Uh-huh. So, what's it like?—to be like a member—the only female member? What's it like?
> ALICE: It's like—it's *okay*. I don't know—like—I always talk about it. I don't know—it's better, you know—I'm the only girl—cause they trust me. You know, I always had their back or whatever—you know—these girls pretend they have their backs, but then—they just turn around and—talk to the enemies—and I don't do that. You know—I know all their enemies, and I don't talk to them and—like—you know—they respect me cause of that—you know—I don't talk—to my enemies.

In stating her preference to avoid hanging around with girls because they are not trustworthy, loyal companions, Alice constructs *herself* as being trustworthy. The girls' personal experiences seemed to reinforce their perceptions of girls as untrustworthy, and their perceptions, in turn, reinforced their experiences, such that the perceptions became manifested as truth. As Brown (2003) notes, being an 'honorary guy' carries the possible rewards of being taken seriously in a world that trivializes all things associated with being a girl. Placed in the larger context of simultaneous gender, race/ethnicity, and class, being an 'honorary member' of a group higher in the social hierarchy carries the possible rewards of being taken seriously in a world that trivializes all things associated with being a Black or Brown girl.

The girls derive their sense of worth from being recognized for their work contributions. This reflects the counterintuitive reality that the girls, rather than simply engaging in delinquent behavior, are actually pursuing mainstream ideals, particularly those of meritocracy. Central to the homegirls' sense of worth is a strong belief in ideals of meritocracy, encompassed in worker-citizen ideals that serve to rationalize the social location of racial/ethnic minority groups. The girls draw upon these ideals to distance themselves from the stigma of their devalued racial/ethnic group. In a broader societal context, similar processes of distancing occur when members of racial/ethnic minority groups rationalize the social location of their own or other racial/ethnic minority groups by attributing it to a lack of appropriate values rather than to structural constraints.

That homegirls' sense of status stems from their perception that they are chosen for their trustworthiness in making valuable work contributions makes sense given the larger context of how institutions function. Historically constructed dominant ideals of worker-citizen are continuously reconstructed at the local level of institutions in the daily processes of regulating its members. The historical construction of citizenship was intricately connected to labor status, and establishing oneself as a worker has always been a critical element for demonstrating eligibility for worthiness of US citizenship (Glenn 2002). The gang is no different. The historically constructed ideal worker-citizen is first and foremost devoted and loyal to the institution and is able to give 100 percent without any distractions.

Homegirls distinguish themselves by emphasizing their work contributions. However, this is not the only basis upon which they make distinctions. As discussed in previous chapters, historical construction of the ideal worker-citizen includes suppression of sexuality and emotions. Homegirls not only pride themselves on being workers recognized for their merit, competing and contributing on the playing field alongside the guys, they also pride themselves in not being romantically or sexually involved with the guys:

> GLORIA: I did so much for them—and they have a lot of respect [for me]. They never tried to have any kind of sex with me. They respect me—you know?…cause I'm their homegirl. Homeboys and homegirls are not supposed to fuck each other. You know?—but some—the girls—
> CARLA: Unless—the ones who have—girlfriends—
> GLORIA: Yeah. But they're not *from* there—they just back it up—but look—some Hoods—some—some Hoods—neighborhoods—they have girls that are from there, but they fuck all the fools from their neighborhood—that's a hoodrat… I'm not a hoodrat—I'm a homegirl. I'm their homegirl—and I have a lot of respect from them, and I deserve a lot of respect. They give me what I deserve—you know?

Being perceived as competent workers not romantically or sexually linked to the guys are two critical distinctions of identity construction for homegirls and serve the basis upon which they stake a claim for respect. This construction also draws upon dominant ideals of respectable womanhood and accompanying requirements of chastity outside of the realm of marriage. This explains why, from many homegirls' perspectives, the only women who merit respect (and thus trust) are themselves and wives. Although current cultural narratives espouse ideas about the sexual liberation of women, this is undermined by the underlying unequal distribution of resources, power, and status. This underlying unequal distribution continues to reinforce the devalued status of women who do not conform to dominant ideals of 'respectable' womanhood.

The girls' narratives reveal how defining self through drawing comparisons to others is a critical element in processes of identity construction. At each mode of incorporation, the girls gain a sense of status through constructing their identities through comparisons with other girls. This is a form of competition for status. For example, many homegirls gain a sense of status by viewing no difference between themselves and women at the top of the hierarchy of women (wives). However, many girls incorporated as hoodrats (bottom of the status structure) also derive a sense of status through viewing no difference between themselves and wives. This is accomplished through their rationalizing marriage as basically comprising the exchange of sex for material comfort. Thus, many girls incorporated as hoodrats label wives as the *ultimate* hoodrats. Defining self through comparison to others is a critical element of identity construction in general, but is more pronounced among those who are insecure about their status. While homegirls drew comparisons between themselves and all other girls affiliated with the gang, the 'hoodrat' served as an important reference point in the talk of homegirls:

> CARLA: So, it's mainly—not that many girls—in your gang.
> ALICE: No—I'm the only one.
> CARLA: How did you do that—how did you—why'd they let *you* in?
> ALICE: Because—like—like my homeboys—they have Hoodrats or whatever—like there and then they just—you know—screw 'em or whatever. And like—I always like—every time somebody dissed their Hood—I—I would jump them or something—and—I always had their back.

That the girls constructed their identities through comparisons to others is expected since in a meritocratic society worth is always a matter of ranking. Competition for status is most apparent in the processes of constructing self through comparisons to others. People understand their positions in the social hierarchy as relative, and it is through comparisons that they locate and position themselves. Previous studies have expounded upon how the self is constructed through gossip or other narrative accounts talking about others. All gossip involves social comparison (Wert and Salovey, 2004). In essence, gossip is a way of attempting to assert power over others. Gossip, as well as other verbal forms of devaluing others, is a way for the insecure or powerless to affirm their self-worth in the social hierarchy (Campbell 1987; Wert and Salovey 2004). Gossip and other forms of negative verbal evaluations have the power to move the object of the gossip to the social margin; thus, it is often directed at those who pose some kind of threat to dominant/institutional ideologies. Talking negatively about others may be seen as a way for the teller to present a favorable impression of self by suggesting that the teller is not the type embodied in the story. Since the target of the stories is inevitably painted as not adhering to acceptable norms, the teller is, in effect, attempting to affirm her/his/their 'normalness.'

Sense of Status versus Actual Status

From the girls' perspectives, being trusted by the guys in these organizations is a valued commodity, of which they are proud, because it suggests that they are one of them. However, the girls' narratives also reveal the distinction between a *sense* of status and *actual* status. One of the most glaring ways that a sense of status versus actual status is reflected is in the fact that the girls do not receive monetary resources in exchange for their labor. Although homegirls pride themselves as being workers, making significant contributions to the gang, they do not actually accrue any of the monetary resources. It is, in essence, an exchange of labor for no resources. Although Gloria has a sense of pride in feeling that her homeboys deemed her trustworthy, her *sense* of status in being trusted versus her *actual* status as trustworthy is revealed when she concedes that although they 'trust' her to carry the drugs, they do not 'trust' her to handle the money:

> CARLA: So, you would hand it over, and they would hand you the money.
> GLORIA: Yeah, they handed me—actually—no—my homeboys already had the money. That's why for sure that shit had to get to—you know? Cause—my homeboys—they wouldn't trust—they wouldn't give you the money—cause it's like—for some reason like—what if I got caught—you know? Money's too important to them...
> CARLA: So, did they ever give you like any kinds of like—uh—I don't know—some of the money or something for doing it or—
> GLORIA: Drugs—they gave me drugs. I never asked for money from my homeboys—you know—like—that was like something that I *had* to do—like—not something that was a job—that I'd get paid for—you know. Like a order—like—something that just basically they—you—everybody has to put in work for their neighborhood. And that was my work—I did a *lot* of work—for my age—I did a *lot*—major work—overtime.

Gloria stops just short of saying 'they wouldn't trust *me*' after previously talking about how much they trusted her and instead changes it to 'they wouldn't give *you* the money.' This pronoun shift is a subtle way of denying that in actuality her status is an illusion. Whereas in regulated markets, labor is extracted for as little as possible to accrue profit, in unregulated markets, labor can be extracted for free. It is not that the values are different in 'legal' institutions than they are in institutions engaging in non-legal activity; rather, it is that institutions that operate legally are governed by structures that ensure a more equitable distribution of resources, etc. (although overall still inequitable), while non-legal institutions lack this regulation—but the two entities operate by the same basic value system.

The girls make sense of their position in the unequal distribution of power and resources in the gang in ways that rationalize the contradictions. This is critical to maintaining an illusion of status. They have to make sense of why they are not paid for their work, and they do so by crafting justifications. For example, although Gloria feels she deserves respect because of the amount of work she contributes and for refraining from sexual liaisons, she does not necessarily feel that she deserves to be paid for her work. She rationalizes this contradiction by making her own nuanced distinctions between work and a job. That the girls value being trusted more than they value being paid speaks to the power of the institution in reinforcing the girls' perceptions that they are somehow the chosen ones and that being chosen is reward in itself. This is the essence of dominant ideals of worker-citizen, infused with notions of the protestant work ethic. To this extent, hard work is not for the purpose of rewards, but for serving a higher good. It is through the work that they demonstrate loyalty and devotion and that they are worthy of the status conferred by the institution. The institution reinforces the notion that conferment of status is reward in itself.

The disjunction between sense of status and actual status is a recurring pattern in the narratives. Indeed, the girls' inclusion is always a pretense of acceptance—it never changes the actual power structure. In moments of clarity, the contradiction between sense of status and actual status is revealed and the girls recognize the discrepancy—at least for the moment:

CARLA: So what's the ratio of girls to guys in the gang?
MARA: There's less girls than boys.
CARLA: A lot less?
MARA: A lot less.
CARLA: And so are the girls—like treated equally in there? I mean they have the same—
MARA: Most of the time yes, most of the time yes.
CARLA: Do the girls call the shots as much as the guys do?
MARA: The older girls do. The boys always have more power over the girls, pretty much. We can have our O.G. _____, which is an old chola girl from our Hood. She can—she can run the shots for the *girls*. And she can run the shots for the *younger* boys. But, it's like, she can't call shots for the—for the people her age, you know what I'm saying— that have—that were from—that grew up with her, you get what I'm saying? Or from her clique, and her time, and you can't—it's like when it—when it comes to your *own*, you know—I don't know—the boys have more than the girls. Always.

Although Mara begins by stating that the girls are treated equally most of the time, she ends up refuting that. Ultimately, the girls realize that they are still *just a Black or Brown girl*, thus void of any real status.

It is noteworthy that she is the one who places the circumstances in the broader perspective of power since I never used the word 'power' in my questions.

As these narratives suggest, crafting a veil of rationalizations is key to the girls' maintaining a sense of dignity, and it is in itself a full-time job because the threads are always vulnerable to unraveling. Although moments of clarity threaten to unravel the veil, time and again the girls make sense of their circumstances in ways to diminish the realities of their circumstances. This can be seen in even the slightest changes in word choices in their narratives:

GLORIA: I just became this drug addict gang member that—was being used and abused by—not my homeboys—but—*for* them—you know—paying their debts with my body—you know—carrying *their* drugs

Gloria changes the preposition to 'for,' as this expresses her belief that she is using her body for the higher purpose of the organization rather than for the homeboys' personal profit. In essence, she rationalizes her abuse in such a way as to not implicate her homeboys. Crafting a veil of justifications includes rationalizing physical abuse as well:

ALICE:—they have respect—like—they treat me like if I'm one of their little brothers. I don't—like we—we get down sometimes and we start fighting for no reason—like they hit me like they hit like another guy and stuff, but—it don't get to me—I don't get mad. And they're like 'damn, what the fuck?'—he goes 'what are you?—a man or what?'—I was like 'hell *yeah.*' I just said—I'm like 'yeah, I'm a grown ass man—*and?*'

Alice reconciles this discrepancy of viewing herself as respected in light of being the target of violence by rationalizing the violence as being a sign that they accept her as one of them. The sense of status gained by believing that she is indeed accepted by them provides the lens through which all associated actions are justified. Thus, she does not feel a sense of injustice that they hit her because she interprets the violence against her as a sign that they accept her as one of them...they would not hit a girl; thus since they are hitting her, it must mean that they do not see her in that devalued category. She gains a sense of satisfaction from the sense that she can withstand or suppress physical and emotional pain, thus embodying the ideal of detachment from bodily processes. In essence, these processes of crafting rationalizations to justify surrounding circumstances are the girls' way to numb themselves to the emotional pain that constitutes the fabric of their lives. It is a way to survive—to keep going.

Another reflection of *actual* status versus *sense* of status is that although homegirls reinforce dominant ideals, they do not necessarily navigate their lives outside the gang with adherence to these ideals. Regardless of their talk distancing themselves from the devalued category of woman, they sometimes call upon the very things they criticize to gain access to resources. For example, since the gang does not provide viable resources, circumstances sometimes dictate that they exchange sex for resources, such as transportation:

GLORIA: I'm walking with this—unattractive White girl—okay—and I'm looking all cute—you know—with my little skirt—back then I was small cause I was a smoker—you know?—and this little skirt—and my hair was long as fuck back then—so guys like that—you know?—So, I'm walking, and I looked cute—in my little sandals and everything... I'm trying to find a ride—finally, I see this guy. He like went back and forth for about—for about five times—you know—looking at me— slowing down, 'what's up *mama*?'—all kind of shit—finally, he pulled over—I was *so* happy—you know?—he was like 'wassup?'—I told him '*wassup*,' so he busted a bitch—he busted a U-turn—he came back, he parked and said 'was*sup*?' and this hyna's right behind me. He said 'you want a ride?—where are you going?' I said 'all I need is a ride right now, I'll explain to you,'...And so—this other girl's like 'oh,'—you know— 'what about me too?'—and I said 'fuck you,'—you know—I get in the car, and I leave this bitch—you know—and she goes 'oh, what about me—what about me?'—and this guy said 'you wanna take your friend?'—I said 'I don't even know this hyna—I just met this bitch right now in the alley. You know she [inaudible] all kind of shit.' He said 'fuck it—you know—if you want to leave her—'—he acted like— she's ugly—you know—'if you want to leave—'—you know—and this guy's all cute and—smelling good with his big old nice truck—you know? So, I'm like—you know—'I don't want her,'—he's like 'oh—if you don't want her, then let's go,'—you know—so, we jammed...we had sex...then he takes me—drops me off at my sister's...

All the things that Gloria usually devalues as a homegirl, she relies upon here to get a ride. This illustrates the contradiction: they know they are devalued as women, but simultaneously know their value as a woman. Navigating place is a matter of navigating this contradiction. Both her characterization of the appearance of her traveling companion and the abandoning of her traveling companion illustrate, yet again, the competition for place in being the 'chosen one.' The girls can preserve a sense of status in these exchanges by rationalizing these instances of trading sex for privileges by viewing it in the context of being the chosen one as objects of desire. This rationalization incorporates a view of their sexuality as somehow embodying power; however, this illusion of power ultimately derives from being desired by the dominant group—men.

Modes of Incorporation Other Than Homegirl

Girls incorporated as homegirls derive a sense of status from making sense of their incorporation as competing on an equal footing and being chosen for their trustworthiness as competent workers void of sexuality. However, girls in other modes of incorporation gain a sense of status through viewing themselves as being the chosen one—or few—by drawing upon a nuanced mixture of ideals of citizenship and womanhood. This section examines the ways that girls who fall outside the mode of incorporation draw upon citizenship and womanhood ideals to gain a sense of status in their gang associations.

Although in the hierarchical structure of the gang, hoodrats occupy the lowest stature, they still gain a *sense* of status through these affiliations. One way that they accomplish this is by rationalizing their sexuality as a way to demonstrate power and strength through the suppression—or detachment—of emotions.

RENEE: But I got like got screwed into a gang, or whatever—which is not good cause then you're like considered a . But—I just thought I was like this hard little (laugh) girl, or whatever—

In essence, her sense of status evolves from the pride that she assumes from being able to withstand the emotional and physical aggression of sexual assaults. Thus, whether getting into the gang by fighting other members (incorporation as homegirls) or by engaging in sex with other members (incorporation as hoodrats), from the hoodrats' perspectives, both demonstrate a central tenet of the ideal worker-citizen. They demonstrate the ability to suppress emotions through emotional detachment from the bodily/physical realm. In this respect, the homegirl and the hoodrat draw upon the same elements in the construction of identity. They both gain a sense of dignity by making sense of their circumstances such that they are, in essence, exemplifying core elements of the ideal citizen—suppression of emotions. Additionally to the sexual aggression that occurs from their homeboys, hoodrats face physical aggression from homegirls as well—as Mara (homegirl) notes, '…we discipline the ones who get fucked on—we just beat them up…' This defies the un-nuanced picture of the girls as simply victims. As seen in chapter 4, members of marginalized groups can, and often do, reinforce structural inequalities through practices reinforcing dominant ideals.

Another way that girls incorporated as hoodrats rationalize their circumstances in a way that gives them a sense of status is exemplified in Renee's story of her eighth grade graduation. Like girls in all modes of incorporation, her sense of status is derived through her proximity to high status men. A man of status (in her eyes) in the gang contacts her. Through these processes, she establishes her status in relation to her non-gang associated peers:

RENEE: My eighth grade graduation. He—called—CK (gang member with perceived status) called me…I'm like 'hello,' or whatever—he's like 'yeah—wassup?—is Renee there?' and I'm like 'yeah, this is her,' and he's like um—'yeah I heard you just got put on the *hood*,' and all this stuff—I'm like '*yeah*,' whatever—I'm just like going along with him, like yeah—whatever—and he's like, 'yeah—you know what I'm saying—I wanna meet my little ,' and woo-

woo-woo—I'm like 'okay,' I'm like 'well, guess what?' and he's like 'what?' and I'm all like 'I have a graduation tomorrow,' he's like 'what—for real?' and I'm like 'yeah,' I'm like um—'I invited almost everybody from the Hood to go—I got passes for them and everything.' I'm like 'I doubt they're coming—*shit*,' and he's like 'you wanna know what?—that's why I'm callin,'—they right here,'… they probly tired—they probly ain't gon make it,'—basically saying they're not coming to my fucking graduation—and my parents were already not going (her parents were on a trip out of the country during that time)—you know what I mean—it was gonna be me, and my grandma, and grandpa. And—I'm like 'oh,' I'm like 'well can *you* come?' and he's like 'fo *sho*—you know what I'm saying—I'll be there for my little *homegirl*,' you know, he's like 'fo *sho*.' And I'm all like 'oh, okay,' he's like 'now when is it?' I'm like 'nine o'clock,'…so—I'm—graduating, I'm sitting down—looking everywhere… cause you know what I'm saying—I gotta show all these little kids, you know, what I'm working with, or whatever (laughing), so…we were walking around…my arm in his, or whatever… and I'm like '*wassup*?' I'm like 'this is my homeboy, CK,' and… I'm like 'you little bitches,'…

By calling Renee and being the only one of the organization who attends this monumental occasion, he gives Renee the illusion that she is the chosen one. She wants him and other gang members to come to her eighth grade graduation so that she can be affirmed publicly since everyone there will witness her association with the representative status symbol (embodied in male authority) of the gang. In essence, hoodrats make sense of their place in the hierarchy in such a way as to accord themselves a sense of status by rationalizing it in the context of being the chosen ones—as objects of desire and viewing their sexuality as embodying power. However, as mentioned earlier, underlying structural inequalities inevitably make the notion of sexuality as a source of power an illusion. The underlying structure reinforces dominant ideals of womanhood, which make it impossible for sexuality to be a source of power for women in heterosexual contexts.

Homegirls gain a sense of status not just by distinguishing themselves from hoodrats, but by distinguishing themselves from girlfriends as well. While girlfriends may make the distinction between themselves and hoodrats, in homegirls' views, there is no difference. From the perception of homegirls, girlfriends are just sex objects who, unlike themselves, do no real work. Girlfriends do not live up to the ideals of citizenship which the homegirls are so proud of and which they strive to embody:

GLORIA: …there's a lot of hynas that they say they're from M. [name of gang], but—they don't say it, but they say they back M. up. You know? But—actually *from* M., there are only three…That's what most girls do—cause their boyfriends are from there—their cousin or—you know—most of 'em, if they're—my homeboys—their little bitches—their little girl-friends and shit like that—back it up because their boyfriend is from that—you know?

MARA: …there are girls that—end up being—the homeboys' girlfriend… she's never put in work for the Hood, she's never—she's never gotten jumped in—she's never done anything for the Hood, she's never backed us up, nothing, but she—yet she's backing it up.

CARLA: Because she was—his—she was someone's girlfriend.

MARA: Um-hmm…those are just *claimers*. Those are just claimers. But it's like—in a way, she's still a hoodrat. Cause—she's a claiming hoodrat, that's what she is.

CARLA: But as long as they're girlfriends, they get backed up?

MARA: Yeah, sometimes. Sometimes—like—regardless—I know most of my homeboys—they never—like they've never put one of their ladies over *us*. You know what I'm saying, they don't do that. No, they don't.

Mara refers to a girlfriend as no more than a 'claimer'—in other words, someone who claims higher status than her actual status. She clings to her own ostensibly higher status by insisting that none of the homeboys has ever elevated the status of his girlfriend over that of any of the homegirls. From the 's perspective, the fact that girlfriends have sex with the men outside of marriage and don't contribute to the productivity of the organization discredits them. However, the actual circumstances are far more complex and contradictory. For one thing, some homeboys *do* make their girl-friends working accomplices. For example, they sometimes use the lighter-skinned girls as 'buffers' or 'walkers' in credit card fraud. While homegirls think of themselves as higher status workers partially because they are void of sexuality, the findings in this study suggest that it is the 'romantically linked' modes of incorporation that are the best avenues to actual resources. This should not be surprising considering that historically in this country, many women have primarily attained resources and status through their romantic links (marriage or otherwise) with men. As Hurtado (1996) points out, depending upon women's proximity to (White) men, they derive dif-fering potential access to status, power, and resources. Monica reveals the possible opportunities to share in the resources that being incorporated as a girlfriend provides:

> MONICA: ...I ended up getting really close to G., and T.,...we used to go out in nighttime—to _____—and steal tools. And like—machinery—compressors and stuff—and then we would take it to this old guy...we used to take it to him—and sell it to him for half price...I started like—having all this money, and they would always give me half price—and I never—touched nothing, I would just *go* with them—and just keep look out while they jumped out the car to do what they were gonna do—and so—you know—they started putting—like—G., starts putting like two, three hundred dollars in my pocket, and I'm just like—oh my god—I started going *shopping*, and I'm buying all this stuff, and I'm just loving it...

Sharing in the actual resources of the gang has larger implications beyond the status girls derive from being 'chosen.' When girls share in the rewards of the resources of operations, a common way to spend the proceeds is to help family members. To this extent, in addition to gaining a sense of status from being 'chosen,' girls gain a sense of status from being able to provide economic resources to family members. As suggested in the previous chapter, being able to provide economic resources potentially changes family dynamics. It elevates a girl's power and status within the family. This is illustrated by Monica's providing money to her mother who is in financial distress. When mothers need the resources from their daughter's activities, they are less likely to attempt to control them. Mothers are less likely to attempt to put their daughters in their place as a child when the fruits of those activities provide some kind of economic benefit:

> MONICA: I hadn't seen my mom—and I—I called her one day...So I call my mom, and I was like 'mom,' I'm like 'can you come pick me up and take me to go get something to eat?' And she's like 'where are you?' And I was like 'you swear to god you're not gonna tell the cops?'...I was like 'I'm at the Motel 6.'...I noticed the whole time on the way to the liquor store, she wasn't smoking, and I was like 'mom—how come you're not—you don't smoke no more?'—and she's like 'no,' she's like 'you know, we're having really hard times with money right now,'—she's like—'I can't even afford a fucking pack of cigarettes,'—da-da-da. She's

like 'no—I haven't been able to put groceries in the house for these poor kids,' and this and that. You know, I'm just—I—just like—it's pissing me off to hear that my mom's struggling—and *I* had *so* much money in my back pocket right there—I had like four hundred dollars on me...I gave her a hundred dollar bill—and she just looks at me like...she didn't ask me about—where I got the money or whatever...I pulled out a hundred dollars, and I was like 'here mom, this is for you,' and she was like—she starts crying again...I'm pissed—I'm telling G.,—you know— 'we gotta go out tonight—I gotta make some money—my mom doesn't have money for the mortgage,' this and this and that—he's like—'well, I have five hundred dollars I could lend her, if you want.'...so I call my mom—'mom, come back.' I was like—you know—'G's gonna lend you five hundred dollars...so I felt all good about it...and that night, I went out, Carla—oh my god—we stayed out from like—twelve—A.M.—'til like—*ten* A.M., the next morning—just stealing...We made $1500... and I'm just like—oh, my god—we're all happy—we're going back to the motel like *hell yeah*—we divided the money. And I ended up getting like $700 of it...because they knew I had to help my mom, so I got a—I got a big chunk out of it,'...so I called my mom—'mom I got the money—so you can go get some groceries,' da-da-da—so she comes or whatever, and I gave her $200 for groceries...never once did I say you have to pay any of this back—I'm just giving my mom money, you know? And with the rest of the money...$50 for N. [sibling], and $50 for H. [sibling]—for shoes—and she's all—you know—like—speechless...And—I was *loving* it—I was loving it...

In contrast to the dynamics in chapter 3 in which Monica's mother aligned with the justice system to turn in Monica, the above illustrates how her mother makes exceptions when she is the beneficiary of Monica's resources. When it benefits them financially, families may not align with the justice system, but instead may look the other way. Monica derives a sense of worth in being able to provide resources for her family ('I was *loving* it... '). The tables are turned, and the child assumes a role generally reserved for adults—providing resources for the family—thus potentially elevating the daughters' power and status within the family. As previously mentioned, girls who navigate as 'one of the guys' do not share in the resources. They are not a part of the division of resources even if it is known that families are struggling. Resources are spread among partners in an organization—not among underlings. These circumstances also illustrate how economic circumstances dictate morality, not the other way around:

> MONICA: one day, my mom calls me, and she's like '*girl*,'—she's like 'the cops just came looking for you,' and I was like 'what?'...And she's like 'I don't know, girl,' she's like 'Do *not* come around the house Monica, do not come around here for *nothing*,'—she's like 'don't even come out of your— hotel room,'—you know what I mean?—'cause they're around here.'

While she may disagree with what her daughter did to gain the money, her mother needs the money, thus the money serves to buy her mother's silence. Whereas before she colluded with the justice system when her daughter would not keep a child's place, now she colludes with her daughter in evading justice authorities.

Although girls incorporated as girlfriends may have more access to a limited amount of resources than those girls incorporated in other modes, they also risk a higher degree of exploitation. Because they are incorporated in the private spheres of men in the gang, there is a greater potential for abuse. This is another dynamic illustrating the disjunction between the girls' sense of status versus actual status. Dynamics surrounding the potential for greater abuse is reflected in the following narrative in which Monica talks about how once when her boyfriend left the house, he locked her in the bedroom:

> MONICA: I remember one time, I was getting high—and—and V., left— so he left me in his room all—but he locked me in—to his room—you know? And I stayed in his room—and—the room was a mess, and—I took it upon myself to clean it—and—anywhere I stayed—like—when I was living with V., or—you know—always—the house would always be spotless. You know—I always took care of things—you know—so, I was just— I was always just like—a respectable person—a—a—a courteous guest, and—they saw that in me—they saw a lot of potential in that in me—you know?—I'm smart—I'm not stupid—you know? I—I respect people. They just saw a lot of that in me—you know—like—I never talked back—I never asked questions when I wasn't supposed to, and—you know—I kept

my mouth shut, and—you know—if they told me to look the other way, I would look the other way—so I never—I never—you know—diso—I would say I never disobeyed them—you know—anything that was ever said—never got around—so they saw a lot of that in me…

In Monica's eyes, this is what she did to earn trust. She kept her place by being obedient—not challenging, questioning, or even doing much talking at all. That she took it upon herself to clean the room while he was gone, because, in her eyes, this is what a respectable person does, suggests how she draws upon a mixture of citizenship and ideal womanhood to rationalize the abuse. The greater potential for abuse also extends to girls incorporated in other modes that expose them to the private sphere as well.

The greater potential for abuse for those girls incorporated in modes situating them in private spheres of guys in the gang is also exemplified in the following. Monica talks about the punishment for a mistake that she made while she was incorporated in the mode of girlfriend (taking the mother of a gang member to a higher up's house, thus violating the golden rule of 'though shalt not give up addresses'). As a consequence, one of the homeboys slashed her face with a box cutter as part of her punishment:

MONICA: …I sit down on the couch—and Ga., just has this big ole smile on his face—he's like 'you screwed up,' and R., comes up to me, and he slaps me across the face, and he's like, 'you fucked up,' you know, 'you stupid bitch,'…he cut me with a box cutter. The little box cutters—he sliced me across my face. You know—the comment was that, that—you know—I think I get a—on—with life because of my pretty looks—and this and that—so, you know, he did that…I ended up—um—R.,—I'm not gonna say he *raped* me, but he was—he forced himself on me to where I just—I let it happen—whatever—you know?…they were making the comments that—you know—whatever—we want, you're gonna do because—you belong to us…they said 'oh, you just think you're so beautiful,' you know, 'you think you can get by in this world with your looks'…so, R., ended up kicking my ass in the backyard—he ended up like really beating my ass—like really, really bad and—and Ga., watched and—and they wouldn't let V., do nothing about it. And so, it was over, and they were like—you know—they called it—a -a- a check court.

In essence, he strips her of one of her greatest forms of capital in navigating competition for place—her beauty. The check court is, in effect, a public ceremony of degradation that serves to reaffirm the unspoken rules, but on a larger level serves to reaffirm the power structure/social order. Ultimately, being chosen means increased surveillance, which may potentially increase chances for sanctions.

Homegirls derive their sense of status through viewing themselves first and foremost as workers who epitomize rationality, reflected in regulating sexuality and emotions. By contrast, girlfriends derive their sense of status through romantic connections with homeboys, although they may still make work contributions. However, some girls gain a sense of status through more nuanced arrangements and rationalizations. This is suggested by Monica's description of her incorporation at one point during her gang associations, not as a girlfriend, but as a 'hostess' for a drug dealer. Although, in many ways, her basic function in this mode was as a housekeeper, she rationalizes her place in a way that confers some semblance of dignity by labeling her position as that of a 'hostess':

> CARLA: So tell me—describe what that was like—what are you doing as a hostess?
> MONICA: It was mostly like—okay, I would clean the house for him all the time. Keep the house clean and cook for everybody that was there—do his laundry—I mean, he would send me to the laundrymat with everybody's laundry—I would do that.... somebody would knock or something—come for something—he'd look out the window and—give me whatever amount they needed—I go down and do that for them, or whatever.
> CARLA: Okay, so you didn't mean hostess in terms of like—during the parties, you would like—make sure there was food—
> MONICA: Oh no-no—nothing like that—no.

As suggested above, Monica took care of the responsibilities involved in running a household. This included housekeeping, cooking, grocery shopping, counting the money, bookkeeping, answering the door, exchanging the drugs for the money, as well as selling them for him. She views all these tasks as signs that she is a trustworthy woman and emphasized in another conversation that she was *not* having sex with him, which adds to her self-idealization as respectable. To this extent, this mode of incorporation shares the homegirls' ideals of regulating sexuality as a critical component of citizen status. This also illustrates how the girls may navigate between modes of incorporation during their course of gang associations.

Incorporation as hostess involves girls exchanging their labor as housekeepers for drugs and a place to stay. The girls begin by hanging out at a house, then end up staying one way or another—sometimes asked to stay by the 'man of the house.' Homeboys often buy their loyalty by keeping them high on the only 'payment' that the girls receive (drugs):

MONICA: He asked me to stay with him…I ended up staying…I just thought—I mean, okay—I'll help him clean—or whatever—cause everywhere I've stayed, I've always cleaned—you know?—that's one thing that—when I was living with V., and [inaudible], I always cleaned everybody's house—my friend Va.,—I always cleaned—so I was thinking, alright—you know—I'll just clean up the house a little bit or whatever, and—I never thought he was gonna—you know?—I never thought I was gonna get that much trust from him—I didn't think I was gonna stay living there that long…before that—I was having to come up with money to get high—so—when I moved in with L.M., it was like I didn't have to worry about anything no more—I was—you know?…So, I'm kicking it with all these guys, and—I'm running errands for them…all the guys would be upstairs getting high, and—you know—they'd get us high and—and then—you know—me and N.—they would send us—to go clean, like—you know, go hook up the house—and me and N. were so high that we didn't care, you know, okay. So, I remember we would clean that house like every single day—cause those guys were so—and I mean—you know—he had me going shopping for him—they would send me—to go do laundry for them—at the laundry mat—oh, my god—I would be there for *hours,* doing laundry for them—and I mean—I was like the maid of the house and—since it was a two story—from his window, you could see who's knocking at the door, and—you know—we had customers in and out of the house all the time, so—you know, he'd give me the stuff, 'alright,' you know, 'this is how much it costs—go give it to him,' and I was up and down the stairs—you know—always doing this and this and going crazy—you know—always running…that house was always packed with different types of people—and you know—I—me being the girl—you know—I—I was the hostess. You know? I think that's why actually he had a lot of respect for me, too, because you know—I never—he could trust me with his life, and I would never—that's one thing to me—I don't steal, and I don't lie. You know—if you trust me with something—I'ma—you know I'ma take advantage of it—I'm not gonna—betray you—that's just—that made me feel good about *my* self. Yeah, so.

Unlike homegirls, hostesses gain their sense of status not in the perception of contributing work on an equal playing field as the boys; rather, in taking care of the daily details of living so that the guys can concentrate solely on work. However, as can be seen, the girls' work in this mode of incorporation includes engaging in a fair amount of the men's business of selling drugs. This, again, reflects the extent to which many girls' association with gangs is in some form of unpaid labor. Like other modes of incorporation, Monica gains a sense of status not necessarily from the position in and of itself, but from the sense that she is trusted, thus in some way part of the inner circle of the high status group. No matter the mode of incorporation, the girls interpret the fact that they are allowed to participate in capacities that seem to entail trust as signs that they have some sort of real status in the organization. Worker-citizens' illusion of power or status is critical to those in power because it keeps workers faithful to the institution and keeps them working for minimal resources.

The disjunction between sense of status and actual status is apparent in that, as in the case of homegirls, girls incorporated as hostesses have limited access to resources. This can be seen when, on the one hand, she says she was on top of the world and that she thought she had made it, but, on the other hand, a few minutes later, she says she was 'like the maid of the house.' Perhaps the biggest indication of their limited access to resources is that during this time, Monica would periodically return home so that her mother could take her shopping for groceries, which she would then take back to the house at which she was hostessing. The fact that she had to return to her parents' house periodically for food suggests that although he was providing a place to stay, her access to resources was limited to the extent that she did not have access to enough food to feed herself. The resources that she did receive other than shelter were primarily in the form of drugs.

As in the case of homegirls, hostesses do not have access to real resources. However, unlike the rationalizations that homegirls use to justify this discrepancy, those in the hostess mode of incorporation justify the absence of resources by simultaneously romanticizing the relationship and making sense of it as an even exchange:

> CARLA: And so—um—was it—when you took the money, did you get to keep any of it—or when you took it, you gave it right away, and—how did that work—did you ever like—get—did any of that money ever filter down to you?
> MONICA: Well like, when I would go s—when I—when I would go sell, it was—I would—like, okay—when I would sell for them—cause I would have my own personal stash, if I needed some extra money—to slang—and that would be my money to keep in my pocket—but when I would sell for them—like on special [inaudible]—I would take everything back to them—it was almost like—I mean—it was a weird like payb—like –you know—he would—buy me what I needed—like—what we call personals—you know—um—once in a while, we would go shopping—you know—and—I stayed high—that's—that was the main thing—I stayed high—I never had to pay for getting high—they kept me high. My [inaudible] always buy—you know—if I wanted to go get something to eat, because—I didn't cook for them—you know—I would cook for them once in a while—so it was always eating out—they would pay for that—it was kind of like an even trade. But like when I counted money for them—it was—*his* money—like [inaudible] and he would give me all the money, and I would count it and—I did everything for L.M.—I was like L.M.'s—everything—you know?—and I handled all of his—I had to handle all his drugs—I took care of his house—you know—I took care of everything—like—a wife—a maid—and a uh—what would you say—like a partner—and everything. I would count his money—he was bringing in like $1000—$1500 a day…I dedicated a hundred percent of my time to him and to what he needed from me. So it was almost like he was my husband—you know, like—every—anything he wanted I would do for him.

In the same way that examining narratives of girls at other modes of incorporation reveals a discrepancy between sense of status and actual status, narratives of those incorporated as hostesses also reveal this disjunction. In romanticizing the relationship, Monica gains a sense of status through portraying it as resembling one that accords her ultimate respect as a woman: a wife. However, her struggle rationalizing the contradiction is reflected when in characterizing the relationship between them—she goes from wife to maid to partner then back to wife ('it was almost as if he was my husband'). Revealing the amount of money that he brought in is a marker of his status, and the fact that he entrusted her to count it denotes her status as one of the chosen ones. Ultimately, she reveals the disjunction between her sense of power and status and actual status when she says '…it was—*his* money.' This disjunction is also revealed when, with respect to Monica's pride in not engaging in sex with the man for whom she 'hosts,' she reveals that he has Monica engage in sex with men to distract them while he robs them. In essence, he controls her sexuality for his economic gain.

Discussion and Conclusion

The findings that girls' actions evolve out of attempts to gain a sense of power and status have profound implications for how we think about programming and how to address the phenomenon of girls in the juvenile justice system. If a motivating factor in navigating their lives is attaining a sense of empowerment and status, then a prime consideration of programming should be devising programs that give the girls a similar sense of status. Most programs fail to take the girls' perspectives into consideration. Currently, the tendency is to view programming as 'if we can only teach the girls that their way is wrong, then we can remedy the "problem."' This ignores that their actions are not a matter of not knowing right from wrong.

The finding that the girls' actions are at least in part an attempt to gain a sense of status has implications for the two most common methods of addressing delinquency and girls in the system: programs targeting changing their value systems and programs targeting 'self-esteem.' Focusing exclusively on building internal elements such as self-esteem is vague and largely encompasses an abstract form of seeing the problem as something that lies within the person rather than in surrounding circumstances. Trying to convince someone that she is worthy despite the surrounding evidence to the contrary is counterproductive. It is not likely that their self-esteem can be improved without changing their status since self-worth and surrounding structures and ideologies are intricately connected. This has implications for 'gender-based' programming as well. One of the shortcomings of many 'gender-based' programs and policies is that they advocate some version of improving self-esteem divorced from larger economic and political contexts. Perhaps gender-based programming could be reconceptualized as status-based programming.

Unless programs incorporate the sense of status sought by girls, they will continue to be largely fruitless. The way to boost the girls' self-esteem is to improve their status in the hierarchy. Rather than focusing on self-esteem as something onto itself, programs should focus on providing avenues by which the girls can attain a sense of status based on accomplishments. This is how a sense of status is achieved in a meritocratic society. Therefore, this should be the focus of programs. The girls need community resources, including programming, that provide a sense of status tantamount to that derived from being the chosen one. Monica's narrative about her position, at one point, as editor of the school newspaper indicates the possibilities when girls have access to other avenues of gaining respect in being the chosen one:

> MONICA: I work for the newspaper here. And they're paying me for that—I'm the chief editor—so. I mean I have—reporters and you know—I give 'em their little jobs, and so—that's cool—you know—I like doing that, and…And like in all my classes—in most of my classes—I'm T.A.—I'm always—the one—like in my cottage, I'm leadership—it—I don't know—it's—I—not that I like being in control—it's just—I like having—I like being looked up to. I like having that respect—that's always gonna be something that I like.
> CARLA: So—how did you get to be the editor of the newspaper?
> MONICA: Because I have the highest—grade in class, and Mr. G. and me really get along, like—J. was the editor in chief before she left—and I was just a reporter, but when she left, Mr. G. gave it to me. And you know—you know—'you're my best girl,' and this and this and that—so I took over it.
> CARLA: So, how does that make you feel?
> MONICA: I like it. I mean sometimes I'm tired because I'll be asleep after school—taking my nap, and he'll call me to go—and it's like—oh my god, I don't wanna go—but once I wake up, and—I like being on the computer.

CARLA: So—and how did you get to be T.A. in your other classes?
MONICA: I don't know—it just—everybody picked me to be their T.A.—
like Mr. G.—when S. got released—he's like 'oh, the job's yours,' and then
Ms. T. for third and fourth. And then Ms. T.—she said because I'm the
only one in her class with marbles in my head—you know—I'm the only—
one that she trusts—and –
CARLA: So, once again, this thing—this—the trust thing.
MONICA: Um-hmm (affirmative). I'm trusted—when they leave—when
they have substitutes—I'm trusted.

In essence, boosting the girls' sense of worth through improving status
means changing the girls' opportunity structures. Providing opportunities
in which they can gain a sense of status, in effect, addresses the surrounding circumstances rather than focusing exclusively on internal elements
(self-esteem). Also, a program that provides avenues for concrete accomplishments is particularly important in mitigating the reproduction of
hierarchies. This is because where there are no tangible products, the primary focus of evaluation processes is acceptance of moral ideals embedded in the institution's notions of citizenship.

Given that the girls' actions are attempts to claim a sense of status
based on core criteria of a meritocratic society, this exemplifies how girls
at the bottom of the hierarchy do not deviate from mainstream values
but cling to them tenaciously. Thus, any focus on building 'self-esteem'
that is not within the context of a meritocratic structure will fall woefully
short. Motivation and initiative evolve from accomplishments afforded
by the opportunity structure, *not vice-versa*.

References

Brown, Lyn M. 2003. *Girlfighting*. New York: New York University Press.
Campbell, Anne. 1987. Self Definition by Rejection: The Case of Gang Girls.
    Social Problems 34(5): 451–466.
———. 1990. Female Participation in Gangs. In *Gangs in America*, ed.
    G.R. Huff. Newbury Park, CA: Sage.
———. 1993. *Men, Women, and Aggression*. New York: Basic Books.

Carr, C. Lynn. 1998. Tomboy Resistance and Conformity: Agency in Social Psychological Gender Theory. *Gender & Society* 12(5): 528–553.

Chesney-Lind, Meda, and Randall Shelden. 2014. *Girls, Delinquency, and Juvenile Justice*. Belmont, CA: Wadsworth.

Fishman, L. T. 1995. The Vice Queens: An Ethnographic Study of Black Female Gang Behavior. In *The Modern Gang Reader*, ed. M. Klein, C. Maxson, and J. Miller. Los Angeles: Roxbury.

Glenn, Evelyn N. 2002. *Unequal Freedom: How Race and Gender Shaped American Citizenship and Labor*. Cambridge, MA: Harvard University Press.

Harris, M.G. 1997. Cholas, Mexican-American Girls, and Gangs. In *Gangs and Gang Behavior*, ed. G.L. Mays. Chicago: Nelson-Hall.

Hollander, Jocellyn A. 2002. Resisting Vulnerability: The Social Reconstruction of Gender in Interaction. *Social Problems* 49(4): 474–496.

Hurtado, Aida. 1996. *The Color of Privilege*. Ann Arbor: University of Michigan Press.

Miller, Jody. 2001. *One of the Guys: Girls, Gangs, and Gender*. New York: Oxford University Press.

Morris, R. 1964. Female Delinquency and Relational Problems. *Social Forces* 43: 82.

Silva, Jennifer M. 2008. A New Generation of Women? How Female ROTC Cadets Negotiate the Tension Between Masculine Military Culture and Traditional Femininity. *Social Forces* 87(2): 937–960.

Valdez, A. 2007. *Mexican American Girls and Gang Violence: Beyond Risk*. New York: Palgrave Macmillan.

Wert, Sarah, and Peter Salovey. 2004. A Social Comparison Account of Gossip. *Review of General Psychology* 8(2): 122–137.

7

Conclusion

The Quest To Flee a Devalued Status

The girls are at the bottom of the hierarchical distribution of resources, status, and power. In this context, they navigate their lives by attempting to claim a sense of worth. In so doing, they simultaneously draw upon and reinforce dominant societal ideals of citizenship (comprising ideals of meritocracy), and thus the hierarchical structure. This study contradicts what others have suggested: that the girls operate with a set of separate values. In actuality, their values are the dominant ideals of the society in which they live. This research supports previous literature suggesting that in a meritocratic society, members negotiate their status through conveying that they conform to dominant ideals of citizenship (Foucault, Goffman, Cooley), which were historically constituted as simultaneously racialized and gendered.

The girls navigate power and status in the institutions that encase their everyday lives: family; juvenile justice system; and neighborhood gangs. In navigating their families, intersecting structures of race/ethnicity, class, and gender shape the girls' attempts to claim status above that of a girl, as well as above that of a child. In doing so, they draw upon mainstream

© The Author(s) 2017
C.P. Davis, *Girls and Juvenile Justice*,
DOI 10.1007/978-3-319-42845-1_7

ideals of citizenship encompassing autonomy and self-governance. In navigating the juvenile justice system, as well as neighborhood gangs, the girls attempt to claim a sense of worth by distancing themselves from the devalued status of Black and Brown girls. This distancing is an attempt to elevate their status closer to the group perceived as best embodying ideals of citizenship. The institution reinforces the girls' attempts to claim this status by setting up a meritocratic rehabilitation system based on ideals of citizenship, regulating sexuality and emotionality, while also controlling any attempts to elevate their status above child. It should be understood that it is not social mobility in itself that constitutes distancing processes. Rather, it is the use of dominant ideas of meritocracy to rationalize social mobility and the social location of marginalized groups that constitutes the distancing processes. These findings call for further exploration of the links between notions of self/identity and broader hierarchical power structures of society. Further exploration of these links will offer a better understanding of the lives, perceptions, and actions of those who occupy marginalized status, as well as of those in power.

The Racialized Origins of the Worker-Citizen

The worker-citizen model, especially how it is interpreted racially, is central to understanding the girls' self-construction within the institutions that they navigate. Acker (1990) and scholars incorporating Acker's theories of how gender is reproduced in institutions acknowledge the importance of race, and class, but fail to move beyond positing gender as the primary organizing factor. Acker (1990) writes, 'The woman worker, assumed to have legitimate obligations other than those required by the job, did not fit with the abstract [notion of] job. The concept of "a job" is thus implicitly a gendered concept... "A job" already contains the gender-based division of labor and the separation between the public and the private sphere. The concept of "a job" assumes a particular gendered organization of domestic life and social production' (149). This assertion neglects the historical fact that the separation of spheres did not fit the reality, nor apply to segments of immigrant women, and women of color who comprised the labor upon which the USA was founded.

While on the surface it may appear that the girls' draw exclusively upon ideals of gender to police self and others, these ideals, to the same extent, reflect dominant hierarchies of race and class. Racial/ethnic hierarchies formed a critical basis for economic and political development in the USA, and as such, are just as much a part of the historical construction of worker-citizen as gender. To understand how these processes are racialized requires an understanding of the material circumstances that shaped the structures and language of meritocracy. Placed in a macro context, the micro practices of these institutions reflect historical processes outlined in Glenn's (2002) 'worker-citizen' paradigm in which U.S. citizenship status is intricately connected to labor status, and establishing oneself as an independent laborer has always been a critical element for demonstrating eligibility for U.S. citizenship for those not occupying a position at the top of the social hierarchy. These processes served to exclude those racial and ethnic groups at the bottom of the labor hierarchy to whom substantive citizenship rights remained elusive. Embedded in worker-citizen ideals is the language of meritocracy developed as a way to rationalize the hierarchical distribution of resources, power, and status along racial/ethnic lines. Thus, any institution incorporating these ideals reproduces race and ethnic hierarchies. Castilla (2008) has revealed the role merit-based reward systems in the workplace play in reproducing hierarchies. Merit is always constructed in the image and interests of those in power.

A Need to Rethink Incarceration

Incarceration, in essence, reproduces the girls' position at the bottom in the broader society. It reproduces their devalued status as Black and Brown girls. As Black and Brown girls, they are not redeemable as are their White counterparts. 'Girls of color and White girls are not playing on the same field when it comes to issues of redemption.'… 'Even if they turn their economic lives around, non-white girls cannot simply assimilate into the mainstream…in this context, full redemption becomes racialized as a privilege of whiteness' (Kenny 2000, 157). In essence, if one does not hold high status before entering an institution which by its very nature is status stripping, it is unlikely that institution will bestow a sense of worth. The girls will not be of any more value when they leave the institution as when they entered.

As in the case of the girls' neighborhoods, the institution itself represents segregated, Black and Brown, low status space without resources. In the division of labor, the institution both reflects and reproduces racial/ethnic and gender hierarchies in the institution, as well as in the broader society. This is reflected in the disproportionate number of Black and Brown residents and low-level unit staff. In this social order, how could the girls not think Blacks and Browns are inferior when they have only to look around them for confirmation? To this extent, how likely are high (or even medium) aspirations to be shaped by incarceration? If anything, incarceration levels aspirations, and, as MacLeod (1995) noted, leveled aspirations are a powerful mechanism through which class (and I would add race/ethnicity, and gender) inequalities are reproduced from one generation to the next. This is a noteworthy consideration given the amount of resources and energy poured into ensuring that the environments of middle class White youths are inspiring so that they may reach their full potentials.

The institution reproduces the girls' positions on the outside by preparing them to take their position at the bottom of the hierarchical structure. The privilege/level system reproduces the girls' position at the bottom by encouraging them to be satisfied striving for basic human rights, rather than material rewards. While the overall flow is one of social reproduction, I am not suggesting an economic or political determinist model in which there is no 'human agency.' However, structure and agency are inextricably linked, reinforcing each other, and agency is never free of parameters or constraints. As Macleod (1995) notes, objective structures shape subjective ideologies, which shape structured actions, which reproduce objective structures. This circular flow of processes results in reproduction of the girls' social position at the bottom of society.

The Enduring Fallacy of the Misinterpretation of the Culture of Poverty Thesis

The state considers the girls to have bad values and designs programs to instill in them a set of alternative, appropriate ones. However, the state misses the extent to which the girls already subscribe to mainstream values. The view that bad values constitute the prevailing underlying cause of delinquency has historical roots in the evolution of the juvenile justice system, as well as in US domestic social policies based on 'cultural' explanations for social inequalities. A pivotal influence on policies was the infamous Moynihan report of 1965, which was based on a distorted interpretation of Oscar Lewis's (1959, 1968) culture of poverty thesis. Moynihan's report asserted that the problem with 'the Black community' is the Black family, more specifically, the lack of 'stable' two-parent Black families. The problem with Moynihan's assessment was not his observation of the fragmented state of disproportionate numbers of Black families, but that he reversed the flow of cause and effect. In Moynihan's reversal, the problem in Black communities was not the social processes that shaped the conditions of disproportionate numbers of Black families; rather, he suggested that the breakdown of the Black family was a primary cause of the disintegration of conditions in Black communities. In doing so, his policy prescription became primarily targeted at fixing the 'Black family' to alleviate Black poverty, and fixing the black family primarily entailed correcting 'bad' family values, passed down through generations and presumed to be the mark of a deviant culture/subculture.

The positing of bad values as an explanation for the conditions of Black families contributed to a social and political landscape in which bad Black values became the primary explanation in all perceived dysfunctional behavior of Blacks and Browns. In short, cultural explanations replaced biological explanations, but in essence became smokescreens for biological explanations, thus ensuring continued location of disproportionate numbers of Blacks and Browns at the bottom of the social/economic/political hierarchy. Nowhere are these cultural explanations more apparent than in the justice system. In fact, however, the girls themselves deploy mainstream values and dominant ideas to police and sanction each other. This supplies an example of the girls enacting state power to impose a definition of the girls' selves that is consistent with state definitions. Dominant ideologies ensure that those at the bottom of hierarchical structures will have an understanding that they are at the bottom because they have not accepted state imperatives. In the state's definition (as conveyed in the ideas the girls used to sanction each other), the girls occupy their social locations because of personal deficiencies resulting from lack of acceptance of core societal (and institutional) values of meritocracy.

Yet, there is a conflicting message in the state's definition: on the one hand, the message to the girls is that they can and should shed their deficiencies and become closer to model citizens by adapting dominant ideals; yet, on the other hand, the state also conveys to the girls that their personal deficiencies come from their innate nature as Black and Brown girls. The irony in this understanding is that since the personal deficiencies are seen as evolving from the innate nature/essence of being Black and Brown girls, no matter how hard they work, they can't really shed these deficiencies. Yet, they are told that the only thing that lies between them and citizenship is their lack of motivation in improving themselves. The proposition that their deficiencies are part of the very definition of their intersecting race and gender status means that they can never truly become model worker-citizens because their supposed innate nature is left out of the very definition of citizen. For the girls, confronted with these contradictory doctrines, there is only one way out. The only way the girls can shed their personal deficiencies is to distance themselves from the devalued status of Black and Brown girls by drawing contrasts between themselves and others who occupy their devalued status. The guys embody, in the eyes of the girls, the very ideals that they have been told that they, as Black and Brown girls, lack: control, planning, achievement, and status.

History has repeatedly shown that a change in dominant ideas evolves from changes in the underlying structure and that it is most productive when it occurs on a scale larger than one institution or program. Thus, the dynamics in this institution are a reflection of the work that remains to be accomplished on a broader societal level. A group's position in the social hierarchy determines the perceived worth of individual members of that group. Dominant ideals of the inferiority of marginalized race/ethnic groups are derived from their occupying a position at the bottom of the social hierarchy. As long as racial and ethnic minorities are located at the bottom of hierarchies of the distribution of resources, power, and status in the larger society, dominant systems of beliefs of their inferiority and accompanying discriminatory treatment will endure. In essence, the hierarchical distribution serves as a constant rationalization and justification of their inferiority and undermines all attempts to think otherwise.

References

Acker, Joan. 1990. Hierarchies, Jobs, Bodies: A Theory of Gendered Organizations. *Gender & Society* 4(2): 139–158.

Castilla, E.J. 2008. Gender, Race, and Meritocracy in Organizational Careers. *American Journal of Sociology* 113(6): 1479–1526.

Glenn, Evelyn N. 2002. *Unequal Freedom: How Race and Gender Shaped American Citizenship and Labor.* Cambridge, MA: Harvard University Press.

Kenny, Lorraine. 2000. *Daughters of Suburbia: Growing Up White, Middle Class, and Female.* New Brunswick, NJ: Rutgers University Press.

Lewis, Oscar. 1959. *Five Families.* New York: Basic Books.

———. 1968. *La Vida.* New York: Knopf.

MacLeod, Jay. 1995. *Ain't No Makin' It: Aspirations & Attainment in a Low-Income Neighborhood.* Boulder: Westview Press.

Moynihan, Daniel P. 1965. *The Negro Family: The Case for National Action.* Department of Labor Report.

References

Acker, Joan. 1990. Hierarchies, Jobs, Bodies: A Theory of Gendered Organizations. *Gender & Society* 4(2): 139–158.

———. 2006. Inequality Regimes Gender, Class, and Race in Organizations. *Gender & Society* 20(4): 441–464.

Acoca, L. 1999. Investing in Girls: A 21st Century Challenge. *Juvenile Justice* 6: 3–13.

Acoca, L., and K. Dedel. 1998. *No Place to Hide: Understanding and Meeting the Needs of Girls in the California Juvenile Justice System.* San Francisco: National Council on Crime and Delinquency.

Adler, F. 1975. *Sisters in Crime: The Rise of the New Female Criminal.* New York: McGraw Hill.

Anderson, Etta. 1976. The 'Chivalrous' Treatment of the Female Offender in the Arms of the Criminal Justice System: A Review of the Literature. *Social Problems* 23: 350–357.

Andrews, R., and A. Cohn. 1974. Ungovernability: The Unjustifiable Jurisdiction. *Yale Law Journal* 83: 1383–1409.

Arnold, Regina. 1990. Women of Color: Processes of Victimization and Criminalization of Black Women. *Social Justice* 173: 153–166.

Arthur D. Little, Inc. 1977. *Responses to Angry Youth: Cost and Service Impacts of the Deinstitutionalization of Status Offenders in Ten States.* Washington, DC: Arthur D. Little, Inc.

© The Author(s) 2017
C.P. Davis, *Girls and Juvenile Justice*,
DOI 10.1007/978-3-319-42845-1

Austin, James, and Barry Krisberg. 1981. Wider, Stronger, and Different Nets: The Dialectics of Criminal Justice Reform. *Journal of Research in Crime and Delinquency* 18: 165–196.

Balck, Annie, and F. Sherman. 2015. *Gender Injustice: System-Level Juvenile Justice Reforms for Girls*. Portland, OR: The National Crittenton Foundation.

Bartollas, Clemens. 1993. Little Girls Grown Up: The Perils of Institutionalization. In *Female Criminality: The State of the Art*, ed. C. Culliver. New York: Garland Press.

Becker, Howard. 1963. *Outsiders*. New York: Free Press.

Beger, Randall, and Harry Hoffman. 1998. The Role of Gender in Detention Dispositioning of Juvenile Probation Violators. *Journal of Crime and Justice* 21(1): 173.

Belknap, Joanne, and Kristi Holsinger. 1998. An Overview of Delinquent Girls: How Theory and Practice Have Failed and the Need for Innovative Changes. In *Female Offenders: Critical Perspectives and Effective Interventions*. Gaithersburg, MD: Aspen Publishers.

Bishop, Donna M., and C. Frazier. 1992. Gender Bias in Juvenile Justice Processing: Implications of the JJDP Act. *Journal of Criminal Law and Criminology* 82: 1162–1186.

———. 1996. Race Effects in Juvenile Justice Decision-Making: Findings of a Statewide Analysis. *Journal of Criminal Law and Criminology* 86: 404–429.

Bowles, Samuel, and Herbert Gintis. 1976. *Schooling in Capitalist America*. New York: Basic Books.

Brennan, T. 1980. Mapping the Diversity Among Runaways: A Descriptive Multivariate Analysis of Selected Social Psychological Background Conditions. *Journal of Family Issues* 1: 189–209.

Bridges, George, and Sara Steen. 1998. Racial Disparities in Official Assessments of Juvenile Offenders: Attributional Stereotypes as Mediating Mechanisms. *American Sociological Review* 63(August): 554–570.

Britton, Dana. 2000. The Epistemology of the Gendered Organization. *Gender and Society* 14(3): 418–434.

Brodkin, Karen. 2004. *How Jews Became White Folks*. New Brunswick, NJ: Rutgers University Press.

Brown, Lyn M. 2003. *Girlfighting*. New York: New York University Press.

Brown, Michael K., Martin Carnoy, Elliott Currie, and Troy Duster. 2003. *White-Washing Race: The Myth of a Color-Blind Society*. Berkeley: University of California Press.

Browne, Angela, and David Finkelhor. 1986. Impact of Child Sexual Abuse: A Review of the Research. *Psychological Bulletin* 99(1): 66–77.

Campbell, Anne. 1987. Self Definition by Rejection: The Case of Gang Girls. *Social Problems* 34(5): 451–466.

———. 1990. Female Participation in Gangs. In *Gangs in America*, ed. G.R. Huff. Newbury Park, CA: Sage.

———. 1993. *Men, Women, and Aggression*. New York: Basic Books.

Carr, C. Lynn. 1998. Tomboy Resistance and Conformity: Agency in Social Psychological Gender Theory. *Gender & Society* 12(5): 528–553.

Castilla, E.J. 2008. Gender, Race, and Meritocracy in Organizational Careers. *American Journal of Sociology* 113(6): 1479–1526.

Charmaz, Kathy. 1983. The Grounded Theory Method: An Explication and Interpretation. In *Contemporary Field Research: A Collection of Readings*, ed. R.M. Emerson, 109–126. Boston: Little, Brown.

———. 1990. 'Discovering' Chronic Illness: Using Grounded Theory. *Social Science & Medicine* 30: 1161–1172.

Chesney-Lind, Meda. 1989. Girls' Crime and Woman's Place: Toward a Feminist Model of Female Delinquency. *Crime and Delinquency* 35: 5–29.

———. 1997. *The Female Offender: Girls, Women and Crime*. Thousand Oaks, CA: Sage.

———. 1999. Challenging Girls' Invisibility in Juvenile Court. *The Annals of The American Academy of Political and Social Sciences* 564: 185–202.

Chesney-Lind, Meda, and Randall Shelden. 2014, 2004, 1998. *Girls, Delinquency, and Juvenile Justice*. Belmont, CA: Wadsworth.

Cohn, Yona. 1963. Criteria for Probation Officers' Recommendations to Juvenile Court. *Crime and Delinquency* 1: 272–275.

———. 1970. Criteria for the Probation Officer's Recommendations to the Juvenile Court. In *Becoming Delinquent*, ed. P.G. Garbedian and D. C. Gibbons. Chicago: Aldine.

Collins, Patricia Hill. 2008. *Black Feminist Thought: Knowledge, Consciousness, and the Politics of Empowerment*. New York: Routledge.

Costello, Jan, and Nancy L. Worthington. 1981. Incarcerating Status Offenders: Attempts to Circumvent the Juvenile Justice and Delinquency Prevention Act. *Harvard Civil Rights-Civil Liberties Law Review* 16: 41–81.

Cruikshank, Barbara. 1999. *The Will to Empower: Democratic Citizens and Other Subjects*. Ithaca, NY: Cornell University Press.

Cullen, F.T., K.M. Golden, and J.B. Cullen. 1979. Sex and Delinquency: A Partial Test of the Masculinity Hypothesis. *Criminology* 17(3): 301.

Daly, Kathleen, and Meda Chesney-Lind. 1988. Feminism and Criminology. *Justice Quarterly* 5(4): 497–538.

Datesman, S., F. Scarpitti, and R.M. Stephenson. 1975. Female Delinquency: An Application of Self and Opportunity Theories. *Journal of Research in Crime and Delinquency* 66: 107–132.

Davis, Angela. 1983. *Women, Race & Class*. New York: Vintage Books.

Dorne, Clifford K. 2002. *An Introduction to Child Maltreatment in the United States: History, Public Policy and Research*. New York: Criminal Justice Press/Willow Tree Press.

Duncan, G.J., J. Brooks-Gunn, and P.K. Klabanov. 1994. Economic Deprivation and Early Childhood Development. *Childhood Development* 65: 296–318.

Durkheim, Emile. 1947[1912]. *Elementary Forms of Religious Life*. Glencoe, IL: Free Press.

———. 1950[1938]. *The Rules of Sociological Method*. Glencoe, IL: Free Press.

———. 1964[1895]. *The Division of Labor in Society*. New York: Free Press.

Empey, LaMar T. 1973. Juvenile Justice Reform: Diversion, Due Process and Deinstitutionalization. In *Prisoners in America*, ed. Lloyd E. Ohlin, 13–48. Englewood Cliffs, NJ: Prentice Hall.

——— 1982. *American Delinquency*. Homewood, IL: Dorsey Press.

Fannon, F. 1967. *Black Skin, White Masks*. New York: Grove Press.

Federle, K.H., and M. Chesney-Lind. 1992. Special Issues in Juvenile Justice: Gender, Race, and Ethnicity. In *Juvenile Justice and Public Policy: Toward a National Agenda*, ed. I.M. Schwartz, 165–195. Indianapolis, IN: Macmillan USA Publishing.

Feld, Barry. 1999. *Bad Kids: Race and the Transformation of the Juvenile Court*. New York: Oxford University Press.

Fishman, L. T. 1995. The Vice Queens: An Ethnographic Study of Black Female Gang Behavior. In *The Modern Gang Reader*, ed. M. Klein, C. Maxson, and J. Miller. Los Angeles: Roxbury.

Fordham, Signithia. 1993. 'Those Loud Black Girls': (Black) Women, Silence, and Gender 'Passing' in the Academy. *Anthropology & Education Quarterly* 24(1): 3–32.

Foucault, Michel. 1965. *Madness and Civilization*. New York: Vintage Books.

———. 1977. *Discipline and Punish: The Birth of the Prison*. New York: Vintage Books.

———. 1978. *The History of Sexuality: An Introduction*, vol I. New York: Vintage Books.

———. 1983. The Subject and Power. In *Michel Foucault: Beyond Structuralism and Hermeneutics*, 2nd ed., ed. Hubert L. Dreyfus and Raul Rabinow, 208–226. Chicago: University of Chicago Press.

————. 1988. Technologies of the Self. Ed. Luther H. Martin, Huck Gutman, and Patrick H. Hutton, 16–49. Amherst: University of Massachusetts Press.

Fox, Kathryn. 1999. Changing Violent Minds: Discursive Correction and Resistance in the Cognitive Treatment of Violent Offenders in Prison. *Social Problems* 46(1): 88–103.

Fraser, Nancy, and Linda Gordon. 1994. Dependency Demystified: Inscriptions of Power in a Keyword of the Welfare State. *Social Politics* (Spring): 4–31.

Freire, Paulo. 1970. *Pedagogy of the Oppressed.* New York: Continuum.

Fujimoto, Naomi. 2001. What Was That Secret? Framing Forced Disclosures from Teen Mothers. *Symbolic Interaction* 24(1): 1–24.

Gaarder, Emily, N. Rodriguez, and M. Zatz. 2004. Criers, Liars, and Manipulators: Probation Officers' Views of Girls. *Justice Quarterly* 21(3): 547–578.

Gans, Herbert J. 1962. *The Urban Villagers: Group and Class in the Life of Italian-Americans.* New York: The Free Press.

Garfinkel, Harold. 1956. Conditions of Successful Degradation Ceremonies. *The American Journal of Sociology* 61: 420–424.

Garland, David. 1997. 'Governmentality' and the Problem of Crime: Foucault, Criminology, Sociology. *Theoretical Criminology* 1(2): 173–214.

Gibbons, D., and M.J. Griswold. 1957. Sex Differences Among Juvenile Court Referrals. *Sociology and Social Research* 42: 106–110.

Glaser, Barney G. 1992. *Emergence vs. Forcing: Basics of Grounded Theory Analysis.* Mill Valley, CA: Sociology Press.

Glenn, Evelyn N. 2002. *Unequal Freedom: How Race and Gender Shaped American Citizenship and Labor.* Cambridge, MA: Harvard University Press.

Goffman, Erving N. 1959. *The Presentation of Self in Everyday Life.* New York: Doubleday.

———— 1961. *Asylums: Essays on the Social Situation of Mental Patients and Other Inmates.* Chicago: Aldine Publishing Company.

Goffman, Erving. 1963. *Notes on the Management of Spoiled Identity.* New York: Simon and Schuster.

————. 1971. The Insanity of Place. In *Relations in Public,* ed. Erving Goffman. New York: Harper & Row.

Gordon, L. 1988. *Heroes in Their Own Lives.* New York: Viking.

Haney, Lynne. 2010. *Offending Women: Power, Punishment, and the Regulation of Desire.* Berkeley: University of California Press.

Hannah-Moffat, K. 2000. Prisons that Empower. *British Journal of Criminology* 40(3): 510–531.

Harper, G., and L. Robinson. 1999. Pathways to Risk Among Inner-City African-American Adolescent Females: The Influence of Gang Membership. *American Journal of Community Psychology* 27: 383–404.

Harris, M.G. 1997. Cholas, Mexican-American Girls, and Gangs. In *Gangs and Gang Behavior*, ed. G.L. Mays. Chicago: Nelson-Hall.

Henriques, Zelma, and Norma Manatu-Rupert. 2001. Living on the Outside: Women Before, During, and After Imprisonment. *The Prison Journal* 81(1): 6–19.

Hollander, Jocellyn A. 2002. Resisting Vulnerability: The Social Reconstruction of Gender in Interaction. *Social Problems* 49(4): 474–496.

Holmes, Janet. 2008. *Gendered Talk at Work: Constructing Gender Identity Through Workplace Discourse*. Malden, MA: Wiley-Blackwell.

Hooks, Bell. 1981. *Ain't I A Woman*. Boston: South End Press.

Horney, Karen. 1967. *Feminine Psychology*. New York: W. W. Norton & Company.

Hurtado, Aida. 1996. *The Color of Privilege*. Ann Arbor: University of Michigan Press.

Joe, Karen A. 1995. The Dynamics of Running Away, Deinstitutionalization Policies and the Police. *Juvenile and Family Court Journal* 46(3): 43–55.

Joe, K., and M. Chesney-Lind. 1995. 'Just Every Mother's Angel' An Analysis of Gender and Ethnic Variations in Youth Gang Membership. *Gender & Society* 9: 408–431.

Jones, N. 2004. 'It's Not Where You Live, It's How You Live': How Young Women Negotiate Conflict and Violence in the Inner City. In *ANNALS of the American Academy of Political and Social Science*, ed. E. Anderson et al., 595. Thousand Oaks, CA: Sage.

Kendall, Kathleen, and Shoshana Pollack. 2003. Cognitive Behavioralism in Women's Prisons: A Critical Analysis of Therapeutic Assumptions and Practices. In *Gendered Justice: Addressing Female Offenders*, ed. Barbara Bloom. Durham, NC: Carolina Academic Press.

Kennelly, Ivy. 2002. 'I Would Never Be a Secretary': Reinforcing Gender in Segregated and Integrated Occupations. *Gender & Society* 16(5): 603–624.

Kenny, Lorraine. 2000. *Daughters of Suburbia: Growing Up White, Middle Class, and Female*. New Brunswick, NJ: Rutgers University Press.

Klein, Malcolm. 1979. Deinstitutionalization and Diversion of Juvenile Offenders: A Litany of Impediments. In *Crime and Justice*, ed. Norval Morris and Michael Torry, 145–201. Chicago: University of Chicago Press.

Krisberg, B., and I. Schwartz. 1983. Re-Thinking Juvenile Justice. *Crime and Delinquency* 29: 381–397.

Krohn, Marvin, James Curry, and Shirley Nelson-Kilger. 1983. Is Chivalry Dead? *Criminology* 21: 417–439.

Lauderback, D., J. Hansen, and D. Waldorf. 1992. Sisters Are Doin' It for Themselves: A Black Female Gang in San Francisco. *The Gang Journal* 1: 57–72.

Leadbeater, B.J., and S.J. Bishop. 1994. Predictors of Behavioral Problems in Preschool Children of Inner-City Afro-American and Puerto Rican Adolescent Mothers. *Child Development* 65: 638–648.

Leiber, Michael J., and Jayne Stairs. 1996. Race, Contexts, and the Use of Intake Diversion. *Journal of Research in Crime and Delinquency* 36: 76–78.

Lemert, Edwin M. 1951. *Social Pathology: A Systematic Approach to the Theory of Sociopathic Behavior.* New York: McGraw-Hill.

———. 1981. Diversion in Juvenile Justice: What Hath Been Wrought. *Journal of Research in Crime and Delinquency* 18: 34–46.

Lewis, Oscar. 1959. *Five Families.* New York: Basic Books.

———. 1968. *La Vida.* New York: Knopf.

Loy, P., and S. Norland. 1981. Gender Convergence and Delinquency. *The Sociological Quarterly* 22: 275.

Mackay, Fiona, Meryl Kenny, and Louise Chappell. 2010. New Institutionalism Through a Gender Lens: Towards a Feminist Institutionalism? *International Political Science Review.* 31(5): 573–588.

MacLeod, Jay. 1995. *Ain't No Makin' It: Aspirations & Attainment in a Low-Income Neighborhood.* Boulder: Westview Press.

Mahoney, A., and C. Fenster. 1982. Female Delinquents in a Suburban Court. In *Judge, Lawyer, Victim, Thief: Woman, Gender Roles and Criminal Justice*, ed. N. Hahn and E. Stanko. Boston: Northeastern University Press.

Mayer, Judith 1994. Girls in the Maryland Juvenile Justice System: Findings of the Female Population Taskforce. Presentation to the Gender Specifics Services Training. Minneapolis, MN.

McCorkel, J.A. 2003. Embodied Surveillance and the Gendering of Punishment. *Journal of Contemporary Ethnography* 32(1): 41–76.

McCormack, A., M. Janus, and A. Burgess. 1986. Runaway Youths and Sexual Victimization: Gender Differences in an Adolescent Runaway Population. *Child Abuse and Neglect* 10: 387–395.

McKim, Allison. 2008. Getting Gut-Level: Punishment, Gender, and Therapeutic Governance. *Gender & Society* 22: 303–323.

Memmi, Alfred. 1967. *The Colonizer and the Colonized.* Boston, MA: Beacon Press.

Miller, Jody. 1994. An Examination of Disposition Decision-Making for Delinquent Girls. In *The Intersection of Race, Gender and Class in Criminology*, ed. M.D. Schwartz and D. Milovanovic. New York: Garland Press.

———. 2001. *One of the Guys: Girls, Gangs, and Gender*. New York: Oxford University Press.

———. 2008. *Getting Played: African American Girls, Urban Inequality and Gendered Violence*. New York: New York University Press.

Moore, J.W. 1991. *Going Down to the Barrio: Homeboys and Homegirls in Change*. Philadelphia: Temple University Press.

Morris, R. 1964. Female Delinquency and Relational Problems. *Social Forces* 43: 82.

———. 1965. Attitudes Toward Delinquency by Delinquents, Non-Delinquents and Their Friends'. *British Journal of Criminology* 5: 249.

Moynihan, Daniel P. 1965. *The Negro Family: The Case For National Action*. Department of Labor Report.

Naffine, Ngaire. 1987. *Female Crime: The Construction of Women in Criminology*. Sydney, Australia: Allen and Unwin.

Ness, Cindy. 2010. *Why Girls Fight: Female Youth Violence in the Inner City*. New York: The New York University Press.

Newman, Katherine. 1999. *No Shame in My Game: The Working Poor in the Inner City*. New York: Vintage Books.

O'Grady, Helen. 2005. *Woman's Relationship with Herself: Gender, Foucault and Therapy*. New York: Routledge.

Odem, M.E. 1995. *Delinquent Daughters: Protecting and Policing Adolescent Female Sexuality in the United States, 1885–1920*. Chapel Hill: University of North Carolina Press.

Odem, M.E., and S. Schlossman. 1991. Guardians of Virtue: The Juvenile Court and Female Delinquency in Early 20th Century Los Angeles. *Crime and Delinquency* 37: 186–203.

Orbuch, Terri L. 1997. People's Accounts Count: The Sociology of Accounts. *Annual Review of Sociology* 23: 455–478.

Pereda, N., et al. 2009. The Prevalence of Child Sexual Abuse in Community and Student Samples: A Meta-Analysis. *Clinical Psychology Review* 29(4): 328–338.

Perrucci, Robert. 1974. *Circle of Madness*. Englewood Cliffs, NJ: Prentice-Hall..

Platt, Anthony. 1969. *The Child Savers*. Chicago: University of Chicago Press.

Prior, Lindsay. 1993. *The Social Organization of Mental Illness*. London: Sage.

Puzzanchera, Charles. 2014. Juvenile Arrests 2012 (DOJ, Office of OJJDP, 2014).

Puzzanchera, Charles, and Sarah Hockenberry. 2014. Juvenile Court Statistics 2011 (NCJJ, 2014).

Quicker, J.C. 1983. *Homegirls: Characterizing Chicano Gangs*. San Pedro, CA: International University Press.

Rich, Adrienne. 1979. *On Lies, Secrets, and Silence: Selected Prose, 1966–1973*. New York: W. W. Norton.

Roberts, A.R. 1987. *Runaways and Non-Runaways*. Chicago: Dorsey Press.

Robinson, R. 1990. *Violations of Girlhood: A Qualitative Study of Female Delinquents and Children in Need of Services in Massachusetts*. Ph.D. Dissertation, Brandeis University.

Rogers, Kristine. 1973. 'For Her Own Protection': Conditions of Incarceration for Female Juvenile Offenders in the State of Connecticut. *Law and Society Review* 7: 223–246.

Rollins, Judith. 1985. *Between Women: Domestics and Their Employers*. Philadelphia: Temple University Press.

Rose, Nikolas. 1988. Calculable Minds and Manageable Individuals. *History of the Human Sciences* 1: 179–200.

Rothman, David. 1971. *The Discovery of the Asylum: Social Order and Disorder in the New Republic*. Boston: Little, Brown.

Sampson, R.J., and J.H. Laub. 1994. Urban Poverty and the Family Context of Delinquency: A New Look at Structure and Process in a Classic Study. *Child Development* 65: 538.

Sarri, R. 1978. Juvenile Law: How It Penalizes Females. In *The Female Offender*, ed. L. Crites. Lexington, MA: Lexington Books.

Schlossman, S., and S. Wallach. 1978. The Crime of Precocious Sexuality: Female Delinquency in the Progressive Era. *Harvard Educational Review* 48: 65–94.

Schwartz, Ira. 1989. *(In) Justice for Juveniles: Rethinking the Best Interests of the Child*. Lexington, MA: D.C. Heath and Company.

Schwartz, I., et al. 1984. The Hidden System of Juvenile Control. *Crime and Delinquency* 30: 371–385.

Shelden, R.G. 1981. Sex Discrimination in the Juvenile Justice System: Memphis, Tennessee, 1900–1917. In *Comparing Male and Female Offenders*, ed. M.Q. Warren. Newbury Park, CA: Sage.

Sickmund, M., et al. 2013a. *Easy Access to the Census of Juveniles in Residential Placement*. Washington, DC: Office of Juvenile Justice and Delinquency Statistics.

———. 2013b. *Easy Access to Juvenile Court Statistics: 1985–2013*. Washington, DC: Office of Juvenile Justice and Delinquency Statistics.

Silva, Jennifer M. 2008. A New Generation of Women? How Female ROTC Cadets Negotiate the Tension Between Masculine Military Culture and Traditional Femininity. *Social Forces* 87(2): 937–960.

Smith, Anna Marie. 2002. The Sexual Regulation Dimension of Contemporary Welfare Law: A Fifty Sate Overview. *Michigan Journal of Gender & Law* 8: 121.

———. 2008. Neoliberalism, Welfare Policy and Feminist Theories of Social Justice. *Feminist Theory* 9(2): 131–144.

Spelman, E. 1988. *Inessential Woman: Problems of Exclusion in Feminist Thought.* Boston: Beacon Press.

Steinberg, Stephen. 1989, 2001. *The Ethnic Myth.* Boston: Beacon Press.

Strauss, Anselm, and Juliet Corbin. 1990. *Basics of Qualitative Research: Grounded Theory Procedures and Techniques.* Newbury Park, CA: Sage.

———. 1997. *Grounded Theory in Practice.* Thousand Oaks, CA: Sage.

Sussman, A. 1977. Sex-Based Discrimination and the PINS Jurisdiction. In *Beyond Control: Status Offenders in the Juvenile Court*, ed. L.E. Teitelbaum and A.R. Gough. Cambridge, MA: Ballinger.

Sutton, John R. 1988. *Stubborn Children: Controlling Delinquency in the United States, 1640–1981.* Berkeley: University of California Press.

Tappan, P. 1947. *Delinquent Girls in Court.* New York: Columbia University Press.

Teitelbaum, L., and A. Gough. 1977. *Beyond Control: Status Offenders in the Juvenile Court.* Cambridge, MA: Ballinger.

Terry, Robert. 1967. Discrimination in the Handling of Juvenile Offenders by Social Control Agencies. *Journal of Research in Crime and Delinquency* 14: 218–230.

Thornton, William E., and Jennifer James. 1979. Masculinity and Delinquency Revisited. *The British Journal of Criminology* 19(3): 225–241.

U.S. Bureau of the Census. 1997. Poverty Statistics on Population Groups. *Current Population Survey*, March.

Valdez, A. 2007. *Mexican American Girls and Gang Violence: Beyond Risk.* New York: Palgrave Macmillan.

Vedder, C., and D. Somerville. 1970. *The Delinquent Girl.* Springfield, IL: Charles C. Thomas.

Visher, Christy A. 1983. Gender, Police Arrest Decisions, and Notions of Chivalry. *Criminology* 21: 5–28.

Watson, Liz, and Peter Edelman. 2012. *Improving the Juvenile Justice System for Girls: Lessons from the States.* Georgetown Center on Poverty, Inequality and Public Policy.

Wert, Sarah, and Peter Salovey. 2004. A Social Comparison Account of Gossip. *Review of General Psychology* 8(2): 122–137.

Werthman, Carl. 1964. *Delinquency and Authority.* Unpublished Manuscript.

Widom, C.S. 1979. Female Offenders: Three Assumptions about Self-Esteem Sex Role Identity and Feminism. *Criminal Justice and Behaviour* 6(5): 365.

———. 2000. Childhood Victimization: Early Adversity, Later Psychopathology. *National Institute of Justice Journal* 242: 3–9.

Wordes, M., T. Bynum, and C. Corley. 1994. Locking Up Youth: The Impact of Race on Detention Decisions. *Journal of Research in Crime and Delinquency* 31(May): 149–165.

Young, V.D. 1994. Race and Gender in the Establishment of Juvenile Institutions: The Case of the South. *Prison Journal* 732: 244–265.

Zatz, Julie. 1982. Problems and Issues in Deinstitutionalization: Historical Overview and Current Attitudes. In *Neither Angels Nor Thieves: Studies in Deinstitutionalization of Status offenders*, ed. J. F. Handler and J. Zatz. Washington, DC: National Academy Press.

Index

© The Author(s) 2017
C.P. Davis, *Girls and Juvenile Justice*,
DOI 10.1007/978-3-319-42845-1

Printed in the United States
By Bookmasters